"There are 37 very good reasons why Herbert Kohl is a remarkable teacher. You will find 36 of them in his book . . . the 37th—and it permeates this moving, tragic work—is that the man cared, really cared." 						—*Minneapolis Tribune*

"The story of an American tragedy . . . Kohl's book goes to the roots of the anguish that grips our people today." 				—*Washington Post*

"What Kohl did in the classroom is really the production of a work of art. As a teacher he was able to do what a million other teachers cannot." 							—*Commentary*

"The story of a modern miracle." 	—*Houston Post*

"Unique in the literature of education . . . reads like a blithe triumph over insuperable odds." 							—*Saturday Review*

"An extraordinary and heartrending account . . . Mr. Kohl tells, with great simplicity and honesty, what it is like to be a teacher in a public school in Harlem . . . all of this is by now a scandalously old story, but it still hurts." 			—*The New York Times*

Herbert Kohl, who began his teaching career in the 1960s in New York City, is now a teacher in Northern California. He has written more than twenty books—mostly on education—and his work in theater for kids has sparked his own interest in playwriting. He lives with his wife of 25 years and has three children.

# 36
# Children

by HERBERT KOHL

*Illustrated by*
*Robert George Jackson, III*

A PLUME BOOK

*In memory of
my grandfather and teacher,
Morris Cohen*

PLUME
Published by the Penguin Group
Penguin Books USA Inc., 375 Hudson Street, New York, New York 10014, U.S.A.
Penguin Books Ltd, 27 Wrights Lane, London W8 5TZ, England
Penguin Books Australia Ltd, Ringwood, Victoria, Australia
Penguin Books Canada Ltd, 10 Alcorn Avenue, Toronto, Ontario, Canada, M4V 3B2
Penguin Books (N.Z.) Ltd, 182–190 Wairau Road, Auckland 10, New Zealand

Penguin Books Ltd, Registered Offices: Harmondsworth, Middlesex, England

Published by Plume, an imprint of New American Library, a division of Penguin Books
USA Inc. Previously published in a NAL Books hardcover edition and in a Signet
paperback edition. The hardcover edition was published simultaneously in Canada by
General Publishing Company, Ltd.

First Plume Printing, September, 1988

20   19   18

LIBRARY OF CONGRESS CATALOGING IN PUBLICATION DATA:

Kohl, Herbert R.
    36 children / by Herbert Kohl ; illustrated by Robert George Jackson, III.
       p.     cm.
    Originally published : New York : New American Library, 1967. With new introd.
    ISBN 0-452-26463-4
    1. Afro-American children—Education—New York (N.Y.)  2. Kohl,
Herbert R.   3. Elementary school teachers—New York (N.Y.)-
-Biography.   4. Afro-American children's writings.   5. Harlem (New
York, N.Y.)  I. Title.   II. Title: Thirty six children.
LC2803.N5K6      1988
372.9747'1—dc19                                                    88-12606
                                                                    CIP

Printed in the United States of America

I WOULD LIKE TO THANK a number of people who made this book possible through their encouragement and belief that my work with children had something to teach others. First there is Jeremy Larner, who initially suggested I write the book. Then there are Nelson Aldrich, editor of the *Urban Review,* and Robert Silvers, editor of *The New York Review of Books,* who published sketches that led to *36 Children.* I also owe thanks to Phyllis Seidel, who took my casual comments about writing a book and transformed them into a real commitment, and to my editor Robert Gutwillig and his assistant, Wendy Weil.

Finally I must thank my former pupil Alvin Curry, Jr., for his contributions to the book and his invaluable criticisms; and my wife, Judy, who has shared with me the joys and pains of working with the children and writing of them.

## THE 36 CHILDREN

| | | |
|---|---|---|
| Alvin, 11 | Leverne, 12 | Desiree, 11 |
| Maurice, 12 | Reginald, 11 | Neomia, 12 |
| Robert, 11 | Marcus, 12 | Gail, 12 |
| Ralph, 12 | Ronnie, 13 | Gloria, 12 |
| Michael, 12 | Pamela, 11 | Barbara, 12 |
| Franklin, 12 | Margie, 12 | Grace, 10 |
| Charles, 12 | Brenda W., 12 | Phyllis, 12 |
| Samuel, 12 | Brenda T., 12 | Kathleen, 12 |
| Dennis, 12 | Charisse, 13 | Shirley, 13 |
| Thomas S., 12 | Sonia, 12 | Carol, 12 |
| Thomas C., 12 | Anastasia, 14 | Dianne, 12 |
| John, 13 | Marie, 12 | Sylvia, 12 |

# Introduction to the 1988 Edition

My first teaching job was in a predominantly Puerto Rican public school on the West side of Manhattan. I started work in January of 1962. In June I received a letter from the New York City Board of Education informing me that I was being involuntarily transferred to an elementary school in Harlem. It had taken six months for me to feel in control of my teaching and become accepted in the lives and community of my students. What I had learned at Teachers College, Columbia was of no use to me in the classroom. I had to watch my students and improvise while struggling to become useful to them.

During that first semester I kept on thinking about how much better the next year would be since I knew the children, the community, and the culture of the classroom. The transfer upset me: I didn't want to leave the children, the community, or my classroom where I lived for almost eight hours a day.

The cause of the transfer was some comments I had made at a staff meeting several months earlier. The principal, who liked to think of himself as a liberal, asked the staff what we thought of the school's reading program. He said he encouraged criticism, so I stood up and spoke out on the lack of coherence in the program and about the outrageous level of illiteracy among the students. He smiled weakly and thanked me. When I sat down, the teacher sitting next to me whispered, "You're not going to be here next year." She was right.

Involuntary transfers are not uncommon in large city school districts. They are used as substitutes for firing teachers who become identified as troublemakers and radicals, or in some way may cause embarrassment to the school's administration. Transfer is usually made to a school with a reputation for having an unmanageable student body. The idea is that the students will drive the transferred teachers out of the profession. This happens quite often. In my case I felt like Brer Rabbit thrown into the briar patch. Wildness and the brilliance that often accompanies it offer a challenge that I am still enchanted with in my teaching now, over twenty-five years later.

Children who question, who do not accept uncritically the things they are asked to do by their teachers, are not necessarily bad students or troublemakers. For the most part they are young people whose minds have not been seduced into conformity and whose wills are not broken. If you can reach these creative and intelligent students, you have done what my grandfather called "a job of work," and that is exactly what I set out to do when I was transferred to Harlem.

The first class I taught in my new school was the one described in this book. I set out to teach, not to write about education. At that time I was writing *The Age of Complexity,* a book on contemporary philosophy, and made no connection between my personal writing and my life as a teacher. *36 Children,* which was written in 1966, came about as an act of rage. It took the form it did because I am a pack rat and never had the heart to throw out any of my students' writing or art.

When I came to teach the thirty-six children I was still sad at leaving my old students and yet filled with excitement about the idea of having my first real class for an entire school year. My first teaching experience was with a group of students who had devastated a dozen substitute teachers in the five months before I arrived, and most of my time was spent trying to create some flexible and productive order out of the chaos I had inherited.

Excitement about facing a new situation was quickly tempered with rage at what I saw at the school. The first week of school fellow teachers informed me that the students were not capable of serious learning. One of them told me to single out some boy the other children seemed to respect and bully him for the first few weeks. Then I would be able to frighten the other students and keep the class under control. He even invited me into his class during my break to show me how he did it. Another teacher offered to share coloring book pages with me and advised me that it was just a waste of time trying to reach "them" to read or write. "Just give the animals something to keep them quiet."

The principal promised me that if I kept the class under control for a few years he'd be able to get me a promotion to a predominantly white school in Queens or the North Bronx.

I was shocked, appalled, and overwhelmed by the general cynicism and demoralization of the staff. Of the almost fifty teachers and administrators there were perhaps eight (four of them black) who believed in the children's intelligence and creativity. I made up my mind not to confront the other teachers or to listen to them, for the first year at least. I ate lunch in my classroom, often with the students, and sometimes with one of those eight teachers, but I never went to the teachers' lounge.

After out first year together the children were reading and writing, and had begun to feel that poverty might not be a lifelong and incurable disease. After "graduating" from sixth grade (we had an elaborate graduation ceremony because, as one of the staff put it, "they'll probably never graduate again in their lives"), they went to a number of different junior high schools. During the next few years many of them experienced insult, humiliation, and racism. School had once again become an enemy instead of a nurturing place. I corresponded with many of my former students, visited them at home, and invited them to dinner at my apartment. Their pain and my inability to tolerate it finally led me, four years later to write about our one year together.

I was also driven to write by the academics and educational researchers who were publishing articles claiming that children like the ones I taught were emotionally and culturally deprived, had learning deficiencies, and might in fact be genetically inferior. There was little talk of the effects of poverty and racism, no finger-pointing at school officials who scorned the children or at the society that found them dispensable. The children were blamed for the failures of their teachers and of the system that paid people who simply could not serve the community they worked in. There was no talk of radical change in the economic and social order that was punishing the children and their families or in the pedagogy that was simply and unambiguously failing. So I decided to write about what happened in my class and let my students' voices, much more persuasive than mine, tell their story.

In *36 Children* I wanted to demonstrate that the myth that educational failure was the children's fault was both false and dangerous. I chose a story form rather than writing a scholarly treatise because I was writing for my students, their parents, and other decent people who cared about social and economic justice. I wanted to make a book that could be read by anyone and not a textbook.

What has happened to the thirty-six children since 1962? They were twelve years old then, and now, those who have survived (at least two have died) are in their mid-thirties. Four are schoolteachers. A number are artists, one a filmmaker. Two work in the television industry. One works for the telephone company, one for a bank, and two are executive secretaries. Some are on the streets doing what-ever they can. The girls seem to be doing better than the boys. The ones who are married have children who are as old as they were when we were together. I've not heard from or about half of them.

I think a lot about the children of my former students. Some of them will have better opportunities than if they were growing up in Harlem in the early 1960s, and some of them, if they are still in the neighborhoods the kids used to call "junkies' paradise," will have hardly a chance at all. The schools like the one I taught in are, if anything, in worse shape. It has been an indifferent time. "Benign neglect"—that is, turning away from decency and social responsibility—has been characteristic of the last eight years, and has been nothing but a mask for racism. There was some hope in the late sixties and the seventies that education could become a force for permanent social change and that economic equality would emerge from educational equality. It hasn't turned out that way.

Educational dialogue in the United States these days focuses on "excellence," a euphemism for elitism, for serving the privileged and ignoring the poor. It also focuses on obedience, market skills, and the aggrandizement of Western culture. The Reagan years of free-market economics, cuts in government spending, and obeisance to conservative bullies and fanatic fundamentalists in educational matters have undone a lot of good work. Often this immorality is defended in the mythical "national interest" and the "defense of freedom." Instead the interest of the nation is what must be considered, of all of the people and all of their children, and freedom is only real when people are able to care about more than their own needs.

There are hints, though, of a resurgence of concern for decency and a tolerance for openness and compassion. Many school people throughout the country have begun to discover, once again, that getting tough does not make good students. Choice, the focus on the interests of students and the comfort of their learning environment— that is, respect for the young and concern for their future—can be found in many classrooms. There are also urban schools, ghetto schools, where each student is treated with a care and love that she or he deserves. In education, as well as in politics, it is possible that a new level of educational progressivism as well as a new political and social climate might be developing. It is possible that all of the cultures of the world might become respected in the curriculum, and that a new generation of young and romantic teachers will join with those of us who have been around for a while to reassert, in our classrooms and in the community, the idea that each and every child has unknown and unpredictable potential. It is possible that inequality will become a topic of study and social action an integral part of young people's school life. The past might be studied in order to transform the present in ways that lead not merely to personal growth, but to community growth and economic as well as social democracy.

The ideas that drove my teaching in the sixties were political and moral as well as pedagogic, and I still hold the belief that democratic, people-oriented socialism is the only decent way to live. And

cautiously, with trepidation, I have a little bit of hope that I might
see another time of hope, as we saw in the sixties, over the next
decade. After all, if an idea is unpopular for a time, that doesn't
mean it's wrong.

And yet the children continue to hurt and to be magical. Last year
I worked with a group of five-to-ten-year-olds and found them as
exciting, complex, and creative as any I've taught. This year my
students are in high school and once again I've learned as much as
I've taught. Each group of young people is new and can make the
world new if given love and the shared resources of a caring
community.

What I learned from teaching the thirty-six children was to distrust
preconceptions about what it is possible for young people to do. In
my experience all children are strong in their own ways. Children
who fail, whose lives are miserable, are made that way in and out of
school because of some form of injustice. For that reason fundamental change has to take place in school, and in society as well, so that
beautiful lives are not wasted. Every teacher has a responsibility, as
a craftsperson, to hone her or his skills and refuse to believe there is
one child destined to failure. Similarly, every teacher has a responsibility, as a citizen, to act politically in the name of his or her
students for the creation of a just world where children can do
rewarding work and live happy lives. If that means being criticized
by administrators, becoming involuntarily transferred or even fired,
one should be proud of being a troublemaker in a troubled world.

*Note:* When I wrote *36 Children* the word "negro" was a com-
monly accepted term and the word "black" was used in the community in a perjorative way. Therefore in the text I used "negro,"
although now I would use "black."

—HERBERT KOHL
*Point Arena, Calif.*
*March 1988*

# PART ONE

# *Teaching*

I cannot bring a world quite round,
Although I patch it as I can.

I sing a hero's head, large eye
And bearded bronze, but not a man,

Although I patch him as I can
And reach through him almost to man.

If to serenade almost to man
Is to miss, by that, things as they are,

Say that it is the serenade
Of a man that plays a blue guitar.

WALLACE STEVENS
*The Man with the Blue Guitar*

MY ALARM CLOCK rang at seven thirty, but I was up and dressed at seven. It was only a fifteen-minute bus ride from my apartment on 90th Street and Madison Avenue to the school on 119th Street and Madison.

There had been an orientation session the day before. I remembered the principal's words. "In times like these, this is the most exciting place to be, in the midst of ferment and creative activity. Never has teaching offered such opportunities . . . we are together here in a difficult situation. They are not the easiest children, yet the rewards are so great—a smile, loving concern, what an inspiration, a felicitous experience."

I remembered my barren classroom, no books, a battered piano, broken windows and desks, falling plaster, and an oppressive darkness.

I was handed a roll book with thirty-six names and thirty-six cumulative record cards, years of judgments already passed upon the children, their official personalities. I read through the names, twenty girls and sixteen boys, the 6-1 class, though I was supposed to be teaching the fifth grade and had planned for it all summer. Then I locked the record cards away in the closet. The children would tell me who they were. Each child, each new school year, is potentially many things, only one of which the cumulative record card documents. It is amazing how "emotional" problems can disappear, how the dullest child can be transformed into the keenest and the brightest into the most ordinary when the prefabricated judgments of other teachers are forgotten.

The children entered at nine and filled up the seats. They were silent and stared at me. It was a shock to see thirty-six black faces before me. No preparation helped. It is one thing to be liberal and talk, another to face something and learn that you're afraid.

The children sat quietly, expectant. *Everything must go well; we must like each other.*

Hands went up as I called the roll. Anxious faces, hostile, indifferent, weary of the ritual, confident of its outcome.

13

The smartest class in the sixth grade, yet no books.

"Write about yourselves, tell me who you are." (I hadn't said who I was, too nervous.)

Slowly they set to work, the first directions followed— and if they had refused?

Then arithmetic, the children working silently, a sullen, impenetrable front. *To talk to them, to open them up this first day.*

"What would you like to learn this year? My name is Mr. Kohl."

Silence, the children looked up at me with expressionless faces, thirty-six of them crowded at thirty-five broken desks. *This is the smartest class?*

*Explain: they're old enough to choose, enough time to learn what they'd like as well as what they have to.*

Silence, a restless movement rippled through the class. *Don't they understand? There must be something that inter-. ests them, that they care to know more about.*

A hand shot up in the corner of the room.

"I want to learn more about volcanoes. What are volcanoes?"

The class seemed interested. I sketched a volcano on the blackboard, made a few comments, and promised to return.

"Anything else? Anyone else interested in something?"

Silence, then the same hand.

"Why do volcanoes form?"

And during the answer:

"Why don't we have a volcano here?"

A contest. The class savored it, I accepted. Question, response, question. I walked toward my inquisitor, studying his mischievous eyes, possessed and possessing smile. I moved to congratulate him, my hand went happily toward his shoulder. I dared because I was afraid.

His hands shot up to protect his dark face, eyes contracted in fear, body coiled ready to bolt for the door and out, down the stairs into the streets.

"But why should I hit you?"

*They're afraid too!*

Hands relaxed, he looked torn and puzzled. I changed the subject quickly and moved on to social studies—How We Became Modern America.

"Who remembers what America was like in 1800?"

A few children laughed; the rest barely looked at me.

"Can anyone tell me what was going on about 1800? Remember, you studied it last year. Why don't we start more specifically? What do you think you'd see if you walked down Madison Avenue in those days?"

A lovely hand, almost too thin to be seen, tentatively rose. "Cars?"

"Do you think there were cars in 1800? Remember that was over a hundred and fifty years ago. Think of what you learned last year and try again. Do you think there were cars then?"

"Yes . . . no . . . I don't know."

She withdrew, and the class became restless as my anger rose.

At last another hand.

"Grass and trees?"

The class broke up as I tried to contain my frustration.

"I don't know what you're laughing about—it's the right answer. In those days Harlem was farmland with fields and trees and a few houses. There weren't any roads or houses like the ones outside, or street lights or electricity. There probably wasn't even a Madison Avenue."

The class was outraged. It was inconceivable to them that there was a time their Harlem didn't exist.

"Stop this noise and let's think. Do you believe that Harlem was here a thousand years ago?"

A pause, several uncertain Noes.

"It's possible that the land was green then. Why couldn't Harlem also have been green a hundred and fifty or two hundred years ago?"

No response. The weight of Harlem and my whiteness and strangeness hung in the air as I droned on, lost in my righteous monologue. The uproar turned into sullen silence. A slow nervous drumming began at several desks; the atmosphere closed as intelligent faces lost their animation. Yet I didn't understand my mistake, the children's rejection of me and my ideas. Nothing worked, I tried to joke, command, play—the children remained joyless until the bell, then quietly left for lunch.

There was an hour to summon energy and prepare for the afternoon, yet it seemed futile. What good are plans, clever new methods and materials, when the children didn't— wouldn't—care or listen? Perhaps the best solution was to prepare for hostility and silence, become the cynical teacher, untaught by his pupils, ungiving himself, yet protected.

At one o'clock, my tentative cynicism assumed, I found myself once again unprepared for the children who returned and noisily and boisterously avoided me. Running, playing, fighting—they were alive as they tore about the room. I was relieved, yet how to establish order? I fell back on teacherly words.

"You've had enough time to run around. Everybody please go to your seats. We have work to begin."

No response. The boy who had been so scared during the morning was flying across the back of the room pursued by a demonic-looking child wearing black glasses. Girls stood gossiping in little groups, a tall boy fantasized before four admiring listeners, while a few children wandered in and out of the room. I still knew no one's name.

"Sit down, we've got to work. At three o'clock you can talk all you want to."

One timid girl listened. I prepared to use one of the teacher's most fearsome weapons and last resources. Quickly white paper was on my desk, the blackboard erased, and numbers from 1 to 10 and 11 to 20 appeared neatly in two columns.

"We're now going to have an *important* spelling test. Please, young lady"—I selected one of the gossipers—"what's your name? Neomia, pass out the paper. When you get your paper, fold it in half, put your heading on it, and number carefully from one to ten and eleven to twenty, exactly as you see it on the blackboard."

Reluctantly the girls responded, then a few boys, until after the fourth, weariest, repetition of the directions the class was seated and ready to begin—I thought.

Rip, a crumpled paper flew onto the floor. Quickly I replaced it; things had to get moving.

Rip, another paper, rip. I got the rhythm and began quickly, silently replacing crumpled papers.

"The first word is *anchor*. The ship dropped an *anchor*. Anchor."

"A what?"

"Where?"

"Number two is *final*. *Final* means last, *final*. Number three is *decision*. He couldn't make a *decision* quickly enough."

"What *decision*?"

"What was number two?"

"*Final*."

I was trapped.

"Then what was number one?"

"*Anchor*."

"I missed a word."

"Number four is *reason*. What is the *reason* for all this noise?"

"Because it's the first day of school."

"Yeah, this is too hard for the first day."

"We'll go on without any comments whatever. The next word is ——"

"What number is it?"

"—— direction. What *direction* are we going? *Direction*."

"What's four?"

The test seemed endless, but it did end at two o'clock. What next? Once more I needed to regain my strength and composure, and it was still the first day.

"Mr. Kohl, can we please talk to each other about the summer? We won't play around. Please, it's only the first day."

"I'll tell you what, you can talk, but on the condition that everyone, I mean *every single person in the room*, keeps quiet for one whole minute."

Teacher still had to show he was strong. To prove what? The children succeeded in remaining silent on the third attempt; they proved they could listen. Triumphant, I tried more.

"Now let's try for thirty seconds to think of one color."

"You said we could talk!"

"My head hurts, I don't want to think anymore."

"It's not fair!"

It wasn't. A solid mass of resistance coagulated, frustrating my need to command. The children would not be moved.

"You're right, I'm sorry. Take ten minutes to talk and then we'll get back to work."

For ten minutes the children talked quietly; there was time to prepare for the last half hour. I looked over my lesson plans: Reading, 9 to 10; Social Studies, 10 to 10:45, etc., etc. How absurd academic time was in the face of the real day. *Where to look?*

"You like it here, Mr. Kohl?"

I looked up into a lovely sad face.

"What do you mean?"

"I mean do you like it here, Mr. Kohl, what are you teaching us for?"

*What?*

"Well, I . . . not now. Maybe you can see me at three and we can talk. The class has to get back to work. All right, everybody back to your seats, get ready to work."

She had her answer and sat down and waited with the rest of the class. They were satisfied with the bargain. Only it was I who failed then; exhausted, demoralized, I only wanted three o'clock to arrive.

"It's almost three o'clock and we don't have much time left."

I dragged the words out, listening only for the bell.

"This is only the first day, and of course we haven't got much done. I expect more from you during the year . . ."

The class sensed the maneuver and fell nervous again.

"Take out your notebooks and open to a clean page. Each day except Friday you'll get homework."

My words weighed heavy and false; it wasn't my voice but some common tyrant or moralizer, a tired old man speaking.

"There are many things I'm not strict about but homework is the one thing I insist upon. In my class *everybody always* does homework. I will check your work every morning. Now copy the assignment I'm putting on the blackboard, and then when you're finished, please line up in the back of the room."

*What assignment? What lie now?* I turned to the blackboard, groping for something to draw the children closer to me, for something to let them know I cared. *I did care!*

"Draw a picture of your home, the room you live in. Put in all the furniture, the TV, the windows and doors. You don't have to do it in any special way but keep in mind that the main purpose of the picture should be to show someone what your house looks like."

The children laughed, pointed, then a hand rose, a hand I couldn't attach to a body or face. They all looked alike. I felt sad, lonely.

"Do you have to show your house?"

Two boys snickered. *Are there children ashamed to describe their homes?—have I misunderstood again?* The voice in me answered again.

"Yes."

"I mean . . . what if you can't draw, can you let someone help you?"

"Yes, if you can explain the drawing yourself."

"What if your brother can't draw?"

"Then write a description of your apartment. Remember, *everybody always* does homework in my classes."

The class copied the assignment and lined up, first collecting everything they'd brought with them. The room was as empty as it was at eight o'clock. Tired, weary of discipline, authority, school itself, I rushed the class down the stairs and into the street in some unacknowledged state of disorder.

The bedlam on 119th Street, the stooped and fatigued teachers smiling at each other and pretending *they* had had no trouble with their kids relieved my isolation. I smiled too, assumed the comfortable pose of casual success, and looked down into a mischievous face, the possessed eyes of the child who had thought I would hit him, Alvin, who kindly and thoughtfully said: "Mr. Kohl, how come you let us out so early today? We just had lunch . . .",

Crushed, I walked dumbly away, managed to reach the bus stop and make my way home. As my weariness dissolved, I only remembered of that first day Alvin and the little girl who asked if I liked being "there."

The books arrived the next morning before class. There were twenty-five arithmetic books from one publisher and twelve from another, but in the entire school there was no complete set of sixth-grade arithmetic books. A few minutes spent checking the first day's arithmetic assignment showed me that it wouldn't have mattered if a full set had existed, since half the class had barely mastered multiplication, and only one child, Grace, who had turned in a perfect paper, was actually ready for sixth-grade arithmetic. It was as though, encouraged to believe that the children couldn't do arithmetic by judging from the school's poor results in teaching it, the administration decided not to waste money on arithmetic books, thereby creating a vicious circle that made it even more impossible for the children to learn.

The situation was almost as dismal in reading—the top class of the sixth grade had more than half its members reading on fourth-grade level and only five or six children actually able to read through a sixth-grade book. There were two full sets of sixth-grade readers available, however, and after the arithmetic situation I was grateful for anything. Yet accepting these readers put me as a teacher in an awkward position. The books were flat and uninteresting. They only presented what was pleasant in life, and even then limited the pleasant to what was publicly accepted as such. The people in the stories were all middle-class and their simplicity, goodness, and self-confidence were unreal. I couldn't believe in this foolish ideal and knew that anyone who had ever bothered to observe human life couldn't believe it. Yet I had to teach it, and through it make reading important and necessary. Remembering the children, their anxiety and hostility, the alternate indifference, suspicion, and curiosity they approached me with, knowing how essential it is to be honest with children, I felt betrayed by the books into hypocrisy. No hypocrite can win the respect of children, and without respect one cannot teach.

One of the readers was a companion to the social studies unit on the growth of the United States and was full of stories about family fun in a Model T Ford, the first wireless radio in town, and the joys of wealth and progress. The closest the book touched upon human emotion or the real life of real children was in a story which children accepted a new invention before their parents did, even though the adults laughed at the children. Naturally, everything turned out happily.

The other reader was a miscellany of adventure stories (no human violence or antagonists allowed, just treasure hunts, animal battles, close escapes), healthy poems (no love except for mother, father, and nature), and a few harmless myths (no Oedipus, Electra, or Prometheus). I also managed to get twenty dictionaries in such bad condition that the probability of finding any word still intact was close to zero.

The social studies texts (I could choose from four or five) praised industrial America in terms that ranged from the enthusiastic to the exorbitant. Yet the growth of modern industrial society is fascinating, and it was certainly possible to supplement the text with some truth. I decided to work with what was given me and attempt to teach the sixth-grade curriculum as written in the New York City syllabus, ignoring as long as possible the contradictions inherent in such a task.

The class confronted me, surrounded by my motley library, at nine that second morning and groaned.

"Those phoney books?"

"We read them already, Mr. Kohl."

"It's a cheap, dirty, bean school."

My resolve weakened, and I responded out of despair.

"Let me put it straight to you. These are the only books here. I have no more choice than you do and I don't like it any better. Let's get through them and maybe by then I'll figure out how to get better ones."

The class understood and accepted the terms. As soon as the books were distributed the first oral reading lesson began. Some children volunteered eagerly, but most of the class tried not to be seen. The children who read called out the words, but the story was lost. I made the lesson as easy as possible by helping children who stumbled, encouraging irrelevant discussion, and not letting any child humiliate himself. It was bad enough that more than half the class had to be forced to use books they couldn't read.

The lesson ended, and a light-skinned boy raised his hand.

"Mr. Kohl, remember that ten minutes you gave us yesterday? Couldn't we talk again now? We're tired after all this reading."

I wasn't sure how to take Robert's request. My initial feeling was that he was taking advantage of me and trying to waste time. I felt, along with the official dogma, that no moment in school should be wasted—it must all be preplanned and structured. Yet why shouldn't it be "wasted"? Hadn't most of the class wasted years in school, not merely moments?

I remembered my own oppressive school days in New York City, moving from one subject to another without a break, or at most, with a kind teacher letting us stand and stretch in unison; I remember Reading moving into Social Studies into Arithmetic. How hateful it seemed then. Is it a waste to pause, talk, or think between subjects? As a teacher I, too, needed a break.

"You're right, Robert, I'm tired, too. Everybody can take ten minutes to do what you want, and then we'll move on to social studies."

The class looked fearful and amazed—freedom in school, do what you want? For a few minutes they sat quietly and then slowly began to talk. Two children walked to the piano and asked me if they could try. I said of course, and three more children joined them. It seemed so easy; the children relaxed. I watched closely and suspiciously, realizing that the tightness with time that exists in the elementary school has nothing to do with the quantity that must be learned or the children's needs. It represents the teacher's fear of loss of control and is nothing but a weapon used to weaken the solidarity and opposition of the children that too many teachers unconsciously dread.

After the ten minutes I tried to bring the children back to work. They resisted, tested my determination. I am convinced that a failure of will at that moment would have been disastrous. It was necessary to compel the children to return to work, not due to my "authority" or "control" but because they were expected to honor the bargain. They listened, and at that moment I learned something of the toughness, consistency, and ability to demand and give respect that enables children to listen to adults without feeling abused or brutalized and, therefore, becoming defiant.

I tried How We Became Modern America again. It was hopeless. The children acted as if they didn't know the difference between rivers, islands, oceans, and lakes; between countries, cities, and continents; between ten years and two centuries. Either their schooling had been hopeless or there was a deeper reason I did not yet understand underlying the children's real or feigned ignorance. One thing was clear, however, they did not want to hear about the world and, more specifically, modern America from me. The atmosphere was dull as I performed to an absent audience.

"The steam engine was one of the most important . . .
Alvin, what was I talking about?"

"Huh?"

He looked dull, his face heavy with resignation, eyes
vacant, nowhere. . . .

The morning ended on that dead note, and the afternoon
began with an explosion. Alvin, Maurice, and Michael came
dashing in, chased by a boy from another class who stuck his
head and fist in the room, rolled his eyes, and muttered, "Just
you wait, Chipmunk."

As soon as he disappeared the three boys broke up.

"Boy, is he dumb. You sure psyched him."

"Wait till tomorrow in the park."

The other children returned and I went up to the three
boys and said as openly as I could, "What's up?"

They moved away. Alvin muttered something incompre-
hensible and looked at the floor. As soon as they reached the
corner of the room the laughter began again. Maurice grabbed
Michael's glasses and passed them to Alvin. Michael grabbed
Alvin's pencil and ran to the back of the room as one of the
girls said to me:

"Mr. Kohl, they're bad. You ought to hit them."

Refusing that way out I watched chaos descend once
more. Only this time, being more familiar with the faces and
feeling more comfortable in the room, I discerned some
method in the disorder. Stepping back momentarily from
myself, forgetting my position and therefore my need to establish order, I observed the children and let them show me something of themselves. There were two clusters of boys and
three of girls. There were also loners watching shyly or hovering eagerly about the peripheries of the groups. One boy sat
quietly drawing, oblivious to the world. As children entered
the room they would go straight to one group or another,
hover, or walk over to the boy who was drawing and watch
silently. Of the two boys' groups, one was whispering con-
spiratorially while the other, composed of Alvin, Maurice,
Michael, and two others, was involved in some wild improb-
able mockery of tag. Alvin would tag himself and run. If no
one was watching him he'd stop, run up to one of the others,
tag himself again, and the chase was on—for a second. The
pursuer would invariably lose interest, tag himself, and the
roles would be switched until they all could collide laughing,
slapping palms, and chattering. The other group paid no attention—they were talking of serious matters. They looked bigger,
older, and tougher.

There wasn't time to observe the girls. The tag game

seemed on the verge of violence and, frightened, I stepped back into the teacherly role, relaxed and strengthened with my new knowledge of the class, and asked in a strong quiet voice for the homework. I felt close to the children—observing them, my fear and self-consciousness were forgotten for a moment. It was the right thing. The girls went to their desks directly while the boys stopped awkwardly and made embarrassed retreats to their seats.

I am convinced that the teacher must be an observer of his class as well as a member of it. He must look at the children, discover how they relate to each other and the room around them. There must be enough free time and activity for the teacher to discover the children's human preferences. Observing children at play and mischief is an invaluable source of knowledge about them—about leaders and groups, fear, courage, warmth, isolation. Teachers consider the children's gym or free play time their free time, too, and usually turn their backs on the children when they have most to learn from them.

I went through a year of teacher training at Teachers College, Columbia, received a degree, and heard no mention of how to observe children, nor even a suggestion that it was of value. Without learning to observe children and thereby knowing something of the people one is living with five hours a day, the teacher resorts to routine and structure for protection. The class is assigned seats, the time is planned down to the minute, subject follows subject—all to the exclusion of human variation and invention.

I witnessed the same ignorance of the children in a private school I once visited, only it was disguised by a progressive egalitarian philosophy. The teachers and students were on a first-name basis; together they chose the curriculum and decided upon the schedule. Yet many of the teachers knew no more of their classes than the most rigid public-school teachers. They knew only of their pupils and their mutual relationships in contexts where the teacher was a factor. It was clear to me, watching the children when the teacher left the room, that the children's preferences "for the teachers" were not the same as their human preferences (which most likely changed every week). That is not an academic point, for observation can open the teacher to his pupils' changing needs, and can often allow him to understand and utilize internal dynamic adjustments that the children make in relation to each other, rather than impose authority from without.

After the first few days of the year, my students are free to move wherever they want in the room, my role being arbiter

when someone wants to move into a seat whose occupant does
not want to vacate or when health demands special considera-
tion. I have never bothered to count the number of continual,
self-selected seat changes in my classes, yet can say that they
never disrupted the fundamental fabric of the class. Rather,
they provided internal adjustments and compensations that
avoided many possible disruptions. Children fear chaos and
animosity. Often they find ways of adjusting to difficult and
sensitive situations (when free to) before their teachers are
aware they exist.

Only fourteen of the thirty-six children brought in homework that second afternoon, and twelve of them were girls.
One of the boys, I noticed, was the quiet artist. Here was a
critical moment that plunged me back into the role of par-
ticipant and destroyed my objective calm. What was the best
reaction to the children's lack of response, especially after
I'd been so pompous and adamant about homework the first
day? How many of the twenty-two missing homeworks were
the result of defiance (perhaps merited), of inability, of shame
at what the result might reveal? Was there a simple formula:
*Good = do homework* and another *Bad = not do homework*?
Or would these formulas themselves negate the honesty and
sincerity that could lead the children to find a meaningful life
in school? At that moment in the classroom I had no criteria
by which to decide and no time to think out my response. It
would have been most just to react in thirty-six different ways
to the thirty-six different children, but there was no way for
me to be most just at that moment. I had to react intuitively
and immediately, as anyone in a classroom must. There is
never time to plot every tactic. A child's responses are unpredictable, those of groups of children even more so, unless
through being brutalized and bullied they are made predict-
able. When a teacher claims he knows exactly what will
happen in his class, exactly how the children will behave and
function, he is either lying or brutal.

That means that the teacher must make mistakes. Intuitive, immediate responses can be right and magical, can express understanding that the teacher doesn't know he has, and
lead to reorganizations of the teacher's relationship with his
class. But they can also be peevish and petty, or merely stupid
and cruel. Consistency of the teacher's response is frequently
desirable, and the word "consistency" is a favorite of professors at teacher training institutions. Consistency can sometimes
prevent discovery and honesty. More, consistency of response
is a function of the consistency of a human personality, and
that is, at best, an unachievable ideal.

I've said many stupid, unkind things in my classroom, hit children in anger, and insulted them maliciously when they threatened me too much. On the other hand, I've also said some deeply affecting things, moved children to tears by unexpected kindnesses, and made them happy with praise that flowed unashamedly. I've wanted to be consistent and have become more consistent. That seems the most that is possible, a slow movement toward consistency tempered by honesty. The teacher has to live with his own mistakes, as his pupils have to suffer them. Therefore, the teacher must learn to perceive them as mistakes and find direct or indirect ways to acknowledge his awareness of them and of his fallibility to his pupils.

The ideal of the teacher as a flawless moral exemplar is a devilish trap for the teacher as well as a burden for the child. I once had a pupil, Narciso, who was overburdened by the perfection of adults, and especially, of teachers. His father demanded he believe in this perfection as he demanded Narciso believe in and acquiesce to absolute authority. It was impossible to approach the boy for his fear and deference. I had terrified him. He wouldn't work or disobey. He existed frozen in silence. One day he happened to pass by a bar where some other teachers and I were sitting having beers. He was crushed; *teachers don't do that.* He believed so much in what his father and some teachers wanted him to believe that his world collapsed. He stayed away from school for a while, then returned. He smiled and I returned the smile. After a while he was at ease in class and could be himself, delightful and defiant, sometimes brilliant, often lazy, an individual reacting in his unique way to what happened in the classroom.

It is only in the world of Dick and Jane, Tom and Sally, that the *always* right and righteous people exist. In a way, most textbooks, and certainly the ones I had to use in the sixth grade, protect the pure image of the teacher by showing the child that somewhere in the ideal world that inspires books all people are as "good" as the teacher is supposed to be! It is not insignificant that it is teachers and not students who select school readers, nor that, according to a friend of mine who edits school texts, the books were written for the teachers and not for children for this very reason.

Of course the teacher is a moral exemplar—an example of all the confusion, hypocrisy, and indecision, of all the mistakes, as well as the triumphs, of moral man. The children see all this, whatever they pretend to see. Therefore, to be more than an example, to be an educator—someone capable of helping lead the child through the labyrinth of life—the teacher must be honest to the children about his mistakes and weaknesses; he must be able to say that he is wrong or sorry, that he hadn't anticipated the results of his remarks and regretted them, or hadn't understood what a child meant. It is the teacher's struggle to be moral that excites his pupils; it is honesty, not rightness, that moves children.

I didn't know all of this when I decided that second day to forget the twenty-two undone homeworks and remark that the first homework wasn't that important. I was just feeling my way.

I accepted the twelve homeworks that were completed without ceremony or praise. At that moment it seemed as wrong to overpraise the children who did the work as to degrade those who didn't, since I didn't understand why they did it. They may have done it because they yielded to my intimidation. I let the issue pass, and having the attention of the class, moved on to arithmetic, art, a homework assignment . . . everything was fine until it was time to leave. Half the class lined up, ready and anxious to leave. The other half contrived disorder and puzzled me by their halfhearted fights. Another game of tag-myself erupted. The children who wanted to leave turned on the others, the atmosphere was restless. I wanted to leave too, turned angry, and threatened.

"I'm going to keep you here until you're in line and quiet."

Three voices answered, "Good," threats were passed, and losing my resolve, I ignored the disorder and led the children down into the chaotic street.

I tried for the next six weeks to use the books assigned and teach the official curriculum. It was hopeless. The class went through the readers perfunctorily, refused to hear about modern America, and were relieved to do arithmetic—mechanical, uncharged—as long as nothing new was introduced. For most of the day the atmosphere in the room was stifling. The children were bored and restless, and I felt burdened by the inappropriateness of what I tried to teach. It was so dull that I thought as little as the children and began to despair. Listening to myself on the growth of urban society, realizing that no one else was listening, that though words were pronounced the book was going unread, I found myself vaguely wondering about the children.

But there were moments. The ten-minute breaks between lessons grew until, in my eyes, the lessons were secondary. Everything important happening in the classroom happened between lessons.

First it was the piano, Leverne wanting to play, picking

up a few tunes, teaching them to other children, to Charisse and Desiree, to Grace, Pamela, and Maurice. Then it was the six of them asking me to teach them to read music and their learning how in one afternoon.

There was Robert Jackson. I took time to look at his art, observe him working. He was good, accurate; he thought in terms of form and composition. Seeing I was interested, other children told me of Robert's reputation, and the neighborhood legend about him—when he was four, his mother gave him a pencil as a pacifier, and he began to draw. They told of the money he made drawing, of his ability to draw "anything."

I watched the girls gossiping, talking about records, parties, boys. After a few days, talk of the summer was exhausted. The children began wandering about the room looking for things to do. They seemed relaxed and eager to work then, though bored and restless during lessons. Unwilling to lose this will and energy I brought checkers and chess to school as well as magazines and books. I developed the habit of taking five minutes in the morning to describe what I had brought in. I sketched the history of chess and told the class about the wise man who asked a king, as reward for a favor, for the number of grains of wheat that resulted from placing one on the first square of a checkerboard and then progressively doubling the amount until the whole board was occupied. I commented that the king went broke, and that afternoon, to my surprise, three children told me I was right and showed me how far they'd gotten trying to figure out how much wheat the king owed the wise man.

The checkers provided quite a lesson for me. Only four of the boys in the class knew how to play. Two of them grabbed one set while another set was grabbed by Sam, a tall, respected boy who nevertheless could not play checkers. He sat down with one boy who could play and managed a game with the help of the fourth boy who could play. Within a few days all of the boys knew how to play. The boys also learned that the laws of physical dominance in the class didn't coincide with the laws of checker dominance, and learned to accept this. Over a period of a few weeks the rights of winners and losers were established and respected. During the first few days there were fights, the board was frequently knocked to the floor, and the game was called "cheap" and "phoney." But nothing very serious or extended could develop in a ten- or fifteen-minute period, and whenever things seemed a bit tight I quickly ended the break and the class returned to "work." After a week six or seven boys retained their interest in checkers while three began to explore chess. They grabbed the game, asked me to show them how to set up the men and make the moves, and then they took over. Within a week, two more boys had joined them in developing an idiosyncratic version of chess (when they forgot the moves they were too proud to ask me) which satisfied them very well.

Leverne stuck to the piano and Robert drew while several other boys kept searching the room for something to do. One of them, Ralph, showed me a copy of the *New York Enquirer* one day and asked me what I thought about it. I facetiously remarked that he could probably do better and stick closer to the truth. Two days later he asked me what I'd meant, and struggling to remember what I'd said, I came up with the idea that he report what went on in his neighborhood. He looked at me strangely and asked me if I meant it. I said, "Sure," and he sat down and wrote, though it took him nearly a month to show me what he was doing. The girls were more interested in magazines that I had brought in, and some of them asked me for books.

In retrospect the first few weeks seemed hopeful. I had begun to know the children even though it was in ten-minute snatches; and they had begun to be comfortable with each other, to concentrate on things and move about the class with curiosity instead of hostility. At the time, however, I felt depressed and lonely. The ten-minute periods of some relationship, the occasional sparks of creativity I caught in the children's conversations or in the way they solved problems in their games or social relations, only frustrated me the more. I felt remote, was afraid of wasting the children's time, not confident in my exploration of time in the classroom. Worse, discipline problems developed as the pressure of uninteresting and alien work began to mount over the weeks. Alvin could no longer sit still, he had to be chased; John frequently refused to work altogether; Dennis paused, abstracted, in the middle of something, unable to continue; and Ralph, the boy who wrote in his free time, would walk out of the room, cursing, if I looked harshly toward him. Margie and Carol did their work quickly, then chattered away, oblivious to my commands, demands, pleas . . .

And there was a second line of disorder. Maurice and Michael were ready to follow Alvin; Thomas S., Samuel, and Dennis were ready to follow John. Carol and Margie had their followers too, and Charisse, a charming, brilliant girl, was always on the verge of making an enemy or starting a fight. There were perhaps twelve children who didn't have to be, or couldn't be, defiant.

Each day there were incidents, and ultimately I accepted

them as inevitable and impersonal. Alvin's malaise or John's refusal to work were natural responses to an unpleasant environment; not merely in my class but a cumulative school environment which meant nothing more to most of the children than white-adult ignorance and authority.

There are no simple solutions to such discipline problems, and sometimes it is necessary to learn to be patient and indulgent with a child who won't behave or refuses to work. A teacher must believe that such problems exist in his classroom because he hasn't found the right words or the right thing to teach, and not that they lie in the heart of the child. Not every child can be reached, and there are some children uninterested in learning anything; but they are very few, and even with them one doesn't know.

My first teaching experience was in a private school for schizophrenic children. The children were considered unreachable and actually excluded from the public schools (as they still are, despite passage of a new New York State law requiring public education for severely disturbed children. The New York City Board of Education claims that these children are "mentally ill," not "emotionally disturbed," and therefore are medical, not educational, problems). The teachers at the school didn't have sophisticated medical and educational backgrounds and hence didn't know a priori what was impossible for the children to do. They knew the children as individuals and couldn't believe in children being "unreachable," only "unreached." Over a five-hour day they forgot that the children were "disturbed" and could see them as different and unhappy. At times they succeeded in reaching and teaching those children, in helping them laugh and cry, and become curious about the world.

I knew that, did it, yet when I first began teaching in the public schools, in classes for "normal" children, the sight of a child not working or the sound of a defiant tongue made me nervous, angry, and guilty. The child was "fresh," "wasting time," "defiant," "disturbed," even—there were any number of self-protective labels I found myself using to stigmatize a child who couldn't conform in my class. I couldn't let things be, allow a child not to work or walk out of the room. I couldn't throw an insult off or reply playfully; rather I treated it as defiance, not merely of myself but of all teachers and all adults, an enormous sin *no child ever does in school.*

A child would tell me to get my nigger hands off him, and I couldn't see the pathos and self-mockery of the statement. A confused, unhappy boy would get up and storm out of the room, pleading that everyone hated him, and on his return I would lecture on discipline in the classroom. I would find a child not paying attention and pick on him vindictively.

It wasn't cruelty, though, or human stupidity. I have seen the most sensitive teachers doing the same thing time after time, and hating themselves for it. I remember days getting home from school angry at myself, confused by my behavior in the classroom, my ranting and carping, my inability to let the children alone. I kept on saying, "That's not me, that's not me." For a while, as I learned to teach, the me in the classroom was an alien and hostile being.

But nevertheless it was me, terrified, showing my terror to everyone but myself. I remember one day in September Michael telling me, after a particularly long and bitter tirade: "Cool it, Mr. Kohl. Sam's upset, he didn't mean what he said."

I was afraid that if one child got out of my control the whole class would quickly follow, and I would be overwhelmed by chaos. It is the fear of all beginning teachers, and many never lose it. Instead they become rigid and brutal—everyone must always work or pretend to work. The pretense is fine so long as the semblance of control is maintained. Thus one finds the strange phenomena in ghetto schools of classes that seem well disciplined and at work all year long performing on tests as poorly as those that have made the fear and chaos overt.

This problem is particularly great if the children are strangers, that is if they couldn't possibly be your brothers, sisters, your own children or nieces or nephews. Then you don't know how their parents control them, and it is easy, in the grip of fear, to imagine that the children are never controlled—in fact uncontrollable. It is a short step from there to the belief that the children aren't really human at all but "animals," wild, undisciplined, formless, and chaotic. No animals are actually like that though—it is only human fear that is wild, undisciplined, formless, and chaotic. The myth of children as "animals," the fear that they may be uncontrollable, hangs over all the ghetto schools I have visited or taught in, and for a while it hung over my classroom.

The New York City school system has developed techniques to handle this problem, though so far as I can tell few teachers benefit and many children are permanently damaged by them. A child who cannot conform in a classroom, particularly in a ghetto school, is removed from the classroom, first to the principal's office to run errands, then to the "guidance" counselor, and finally to a special school for the "socially maladjusted," *i.e.,* a "600" school. To help the teacher maintain order the child is removed, yet it doesn't help. In a classroom and school governed by fear, the removal of one disorderly child merely creates another. Fortunately, there are few groups of children so resigned to adult tyranny that they will not generate and covertly encourage one defiant member. Because of this, it was only with the greatest reluctance that I would resort to a class transfer for a child I was having difficulties with, and it was for the same reason I welcomed other teachers' "problems."

I have only known one successfully suppressive teacher. She taught down the hall from 6-1 and had a quiet, rigidly disciplined, clean and neat class. The first week she filtered out into other classes potential "problems," and by the second week, control was total. Her class marched in line, left the building in order, went regularly to the dental clinic, and drew nice pictures. When she retired at the end of twenty-five years, she truly felt she had done many children a great service by keeping them clean and quiet.

Fear is only overcome through risk and experimentation. As I became familiar with the children in 6-1 I became more willing to respond to the children individually and less dependent on the protection of the role of teacher. I let an insult pass and discovered that the rest of the class didn't take up the insult; I learned to say nothing when Ralph returned from pacing the halls, or when Alvin refused to do arithmetic. The children did not want to be defiant, insulting, idle; nor were they any less afraid of chaos than I was. They wanted more than anything to feel they were facing it with me and not against me. These discoveries were my greatest strength when I began to explore new things to teach the children. They were as impatient to learn something exciting as I was to find something that would excite them.

I have never solved the "discipline problem," but I no longer believe it needs solution. Children will disagree with each other and with the teacher; they will be irrational at times, and the teacher will be, too. An atmosphere must exist in the classroom where conflict, disagreement, and irrationality are accepted temporary occurrences. No child, because he defies, should thereby have to become "a defiant child," or because he refuses to work, "a lazy child." Such labeling makes the classroom a harsh, unforgiving place, a world not fit for children or adults.

September 25 was the day of the first Patterson-Liston fight. I had been reading Patterson's *Victory Over Myself* and brought it to school with me. I asked the class if they knew of the fight and they laughed. Sides had been drawn for days, bets made; several of the boys were going to see the televised fight at the RKO, and others defensively claimed relatives and friends who would be in attendance. I read from Patterson's book and talked of the family photograph he tried to remove his face from. We talked of self-hatred and confidence, of the fighters' personalities, of good and bad, winners and losers. Many of the kids wanted Patterson to win, but they were too cynical to believe that he would just because he was a good person. He had to win with his fists.

Some girls felt the whole thing was brutal though they reluctantly admitted that the fight fascinated them too. An argument broke out about the fighters' size and the money involved. I remembered seeing some facts about the fight in *The New York Times* that morning, found two charts, and put them on the board.

The class studied them intently, the first thing they had all looked at so closely all year. They checked off the characteristics and their implications: Patterson younger, maybe faster; Liston older but bigger, heavier, longer reach, stronger . . . Then one boy rebelled and said facts weren't everything, personality counted and Patterson had to be more confident.

### Facts on Title Fight

Place—Comiskey Park, Chicago, capacity 49,000.

Promoter—Championship Sports, Inc.

Time—10:30 P. M., Eastern daylight time.

Television—Close circuit with Chicago and approximate 100-mile radius blacked out.

Radio—Nationwide by American Broadcasting Company (also foreign broadcasts to eight countries).

Closed circuit TV proceeds — $2,000,000 guaranteed. About 4,000,000 expected.

Radio proceeds (domestic and foreign)—about $400,000.

Movie proceeds (Post - Fight showing)—about $550,000.

Estimated gate—$750,000.

Estimated attendance—35,000.

Fighters' shares—Patterson, 55 per cent of ancilliary rights (closed circuit TV, radio, movies) and 45 per cent of net gate; Liston, 12½ per cent of net in all revenue phases.

Prices of seats—$100, $50, $30, $20 and $10.

Scoring—Referee and two judges; 5-point maximum a round.

Return bout—If Liston wins, return bout within a year. Percentage. 30 per cent for each fighter and 40 per cent for promoter.

**HOW RIVALS COMPARE**

| PATTERSON | | LISTON |
|---|---|---|
| 27 years | Age | 28 years |
| 189 lbs. | Weight | 212 lbs. |
| 6 feet | Height | 6 ft. 1 in. |
| 71 in. | Reach | 84 in. |
| 16½ in. | Neck | 17½ in. |
| 40 in. | Chest (Normal) | 44 in. |
| 42 in. | Chest (Expanded) | 46½ in. |
| 32½ in. | Waist | 33 in. |
| 14½ in. | Biceps | 16½ in. |
| 12¾ in. | Fist | 14 in. |
| 21½ in. | Thigh | 25½ in. |
| 6 in. | Wrist | 8¾ in. |
| 15½ in. | Calf | 12 in. |
| 9½ in. | Ankle | 12 in. |

A girl countered by saying Liston was too confident and a big head who thought too much of himself.

After a while the discussion turned to the money and trouble arose—what were ancillary rights, how could you tell what 55 percent, 12½ percent, and 45 percent of the money earned was, could the fighters be sure they weren't being cheated? "Domestic" created problems as well as "promoter." The kids wanted to know who made the guarantee to the fighters, whether it was verbal or written, how much the government took. The questions were real and the curiosity genuine. I answered as many as I could without preaching or handing out dictionaries, without pausing for a lesson on percentage or saying, "Don't you wish you could read now?" The children knew what they couldn't do, and were grateful for the fact that one time in school a teacher answered their questions when they needed answering, and didn't make them feel foolish for asking in the first place.

It was eleven thirty when the discussion ended so I gave the class the rest of the morning off. Some of the children immediately set to copying the charts on the blackboard. Someone borrowed *Victory Over Myself* and a group of children sat looking at the photographs in the book. The morning passed effortlessly and well. At noon I noticed that the book had disappeared, and over the next three months it periodically reappeared in someone else's hands until Patterson must have ceased interesting the children and it appeared on my desk one day.

That afternoon I expected the children to come in as excited and enthusiastic about what had occurred that morning as I was. But it was as if nothing had happened at all. The next day was worse. The children came in sleepy and irritable, wanting to hear nothing of the fight, of school, of anything. Money had been lost, people had argued. Things had happened on the streets the night before—the kids looked at me as if to say "You just can't understand." Charisse actually said:

"Mr. Kohl, we're tired. Let's do reading instead of talking."

ONE DAY Ralph cursed at Michael and unexpectedly things came together for me. Michael was reading and stumbled several times. Ralph scornfully called out, "What's the matter, psyches, going to pieces again?" The class broke up and I jumped on that word "psyches."

"Ralph, what does *psyches* mean?"

An embarrassed silence.

"Do you know how to spell it?"

Alvin volunteered. "S-i-k-e-s."

"Where do you think the word came from? Why did everybody laugh when you said it, Ralph?"

"You know, Mr. Kohl, it means, like crazy or something."

"Why? How do words get to mean what they do?"

Samuel looked up at me and said: "Mr. Kohl, now you're asking questions like Alvin. There aren't any answers, you know that."

"But there are. Sometimes by asking Alvin's kind of questions you discover the most unexpected things. Look."

I wrote *Psyche*, then *Cupid*, on the blackboard.

"That's how *psyche* is spelled. It looks strange in English, but the word doesn't come from English. It's Greek. There's a letter in the Greek alphabet that comes out *psi* in English. This is the way *psyche* looks in Greek."

Some of the children spontaneously took out their notebooks and copied the Greek.

"The word *psyche* has a long history. *Psyche* means mind or soul for the Greeks, but it was also the name of a lovely woman who had the misfortune to fall in love with Cupid, the son of Venus, the jealous Greek goddess of love. . . ."

The children listened, enchanted by the myth, fascinated by the weaving of the meaning of *psyche* into the fabric of the story, and the character, Mind, playing tricks on itself, almost destroying its most valuable possessions through its perverse curiosity. Grace said in amazement:

"Mr. Kohl, they told the story and said things about the mind at the same time. What do you call that?"

"*Myth* is what the Greeks called it."

Sam was roused.

"Then what happened? What about the history of the word?"

"I don't know too much, but look at the words in English that come from *Cupid* and *Psyche*."

I cited *psychological, psychic, psychotic, psychodrama, psychosomatic, cupidity*—the children copied them unasked, demanded the meanings. They were obviously excited.

Leaping ahead, Alvin shouted: "You mean words change? People didn't always speak this way? Then how come the reader says there's a right way to talk and a wrong way?"

"There's a right way now, and that only means that's how most people would like to talk now, and how people write now."

Charles jumped out of his desk and spoke for the first time during the year.

"You mean one day the way we talk—you know, with words like *cool* and *dig* and *sound*—may be all right?"

"Uh huh. Language is alive, it's always changing, only sometimes it changes so slowly that we can't tell."

Neomia caught on.

"Mr. Kohl, is that why our reader sounds so old-fashioned?"

And Ralph.

"Mr. Kohl, when I called Michael *psyches*, was I creating something new?"

Someone spoke for the class.

"Mr. Kohl, can't we study the language we're talking about instead of spelling and grammar? They won't be any good when language changes anyway."

We could and did. That day we began what had to be called for my conservative plan book "vocabulary," and "an enrichment activity." Actually it was the study of language and myth, of the origins and history of words, of their changing uses and functions in human life. We began simply with the words *language* and *alphabet*, the former from the Latin for tongue and the latter from the first two letters of the Greek alphabet. Seeing the origin of *alphabet* and the relationship of *cupidity* to Cupid and *psychological* to Psyche had a particularly magical effect upon the children. They found it easy to master and acquire words that would have seemed senseless and tedious to memorize. Words like *psychic* and *psychosomatic* didn't seem arbitrary and impenetrable, capable of being learned only painfully by rote. Rather they existed in a context, through a striking tale that easily accrued associations and depth. After a week the children learned the new words, asked to be tested on them, and demanded more.

"Vocabulary" became a fixed point in each week's work as we went from Cupid and Psyche to Tantalus, the Sirens, and the Odyssey and the linguistic riches that it contains. We talked of Venus and Adonis and spent a week on first *Pan* and *panic*, *pan-American*, then *pandemonium*, and finally on *demonic* and *demons* and *devils*. We studied *logos, philos, anthropos, pathos*, and their derivatives. I spun the web of *mythos* about language and its origins. I went to German (*kindergarten*), Polynesian (*taboo*), or Arabic (*assassin*), showing what a motley open-ended fabric English (and for that matter any living language) is. The range of times and peoples that contributed to the growth of today's American English impressed me no less than it did the class. It drove

me to research language and its origins; to reexplore myth and
the dim origins of man's culture; and to invent ways of sharing
my discoveries with the children.

The children took my words seriously and went a step
further. Not content to be fed solely words that grew from
sources that I, the teacher, presented, they asked for words
that fitted unnamed and partially articulated concepts they
had, or situations they couldn't adequately describe.

"Mr. Kohl, what do you call it when a person repeats
the same thing over and over again and can't stop?"

"What is it called when something is funny and serious
at the same time?"

"What do you call a person who brags and thinks he's big
but is really weak inside?"

"Mr. Kohl, is there a word that says that something has
more than one meaning?"

The class became word-hungry and concept-hungry, concerned with discovering the "right" word to use at a given
time to express a specific thought. I was struck by the difference of this notion of rightness and "the right way" to speak
and write from the way children are supposed to be taught in
school. They are supposed to acquire correct usage, right
grammar and spelling, the right meaning of a word, and the
right way to write a sentence. Achievement and I.Q. tests give
incomplete sentences and the child is instructed to fill in the
"right" word. Many teachers correct children's writing on
the basis of a canon of formal rightness without bothering to
ask what the children's words mean. I did the same thing
myself.

I noticed that the children frequently said that they were
bad at their friends, or their parents, or some teacher who
angered them. They insisted upon describing a certain type of
anger as "being bad at," and I kept telling them that it was
wrong because "to be bad at" someone doesn't exist in English. And in a way I was "right"; it didn't exist, nor did the
concept it was trying to express exist in English as I spoke and
wrote it. But the children did mean "to be bad at," and meant
something very specific by it. "To be bad" is a way of defying
authority and expressing anger at the same time, as indicating
one's own strength and independence. The use of "bad" here
is ironical and often admiring. One child explained to me that
down South a "bad nigger" was one who was strong enough
and brave enough to be defiant of the white man's demands no
matter how much everyone else gave in. Only later did I discover Bessie Smith in J. C. Johnson's "Black Mountain Blues,"
using "bad" in the same way as the kids:

Back on Black Mountain a child would smack your face
Back on Black Mountain a child would smack your face
Babies cry for liquor and all the birds sing bass.

Black Mountain people are bad as they can be
Black Mountain people are bad as they can be
They uses gun powder just to sweeten their tea*

I think that before we talked about language and myth the children, if they thought about it at all, felt that most words were either arbitrary labels pinned on things and concepts the way names seem to be pinned onto babies, or indicators of connections amongst these labels. These "labels" probably represented the way the adult world capriciously decided to name things. I doubt whether the children ever thought of adults as having received language from yet other adults even more remote in time. My pupils must have found the language of their teachers strange and arbitrary indeed. The "right" language of school texts and middle-class teachers must have seemed threatening and totalitarian, especially since the only living words the children knew and used were the words they used on the streets, words teachers continually told them were "wrong" and "incorrect."

The idea that words were complex phenomena with long and compelling histories was never presented to the children. I doubt many teachers entertained it. The canons of the schools pretend that a small preselected segment of the language of the moment is an eternally correct and all-inclusive form. This form is embodied in basic word lists and controlled vocabulary readers, as if the mastering of language consists of learning a list of fifty or a hundred words by rote. The use of language in human life is continually avoided or ignored, as if it poses too great a threat to "correctness" and "rightness." No wonder then that the children showed so persistently and ingeniously how much they feared and avoided the language of the schools.

Later in the semester I taught the class a lesson on naming, a topic that seems deceptively simple yet minimally encompasses history, psychology, sociology, and anthropology. I put everybody's full name on the blackboard, including my own, and asked the class how people got names. The answer was, naturally, from their parents who made the choice—but not the full choice, it emerged, when Michael remembered that his parents' surnames came from their parents. Then how far back

* Lines from "Black Mountain Blues," words and music by J. C. Johnson, Copyright © 1931, 1958 by J. C. Johnson. All rights reserved. Reproduced by special permission.

can you go? The children thought and Grace raised a delicate question. If the names go back through the generations how come her name wasn't African since her ancestors must have been? In answer I told the class about my own name—Kohl, changed from Cohen, changed from Okun, changed from something lost in the darkness of history; one change to identify the family as Jewish, one change to deny it. Then I returned to the question of slave names and the destruction of part of the children's African heritage that the withholding of African names implied.

Neomia said that she knew of someone who changed his name because he wanted to start a new life, and Sam told the class that his brother called himself John X because X meant unknown and his original African name was unknown. We talked of people who named their children after famous men and of others who gave exotic names. From there the discussion went on to the naming of animals—pets, wild animals, racehorses; things—boats, houses, dolls; and places. The class knew by that time in the school year that one doesn't talk of words in isolation from human lives and history, and by then I had begun to know what to teach.

The emphasis on language and words opened the children to the whole process of verbal communication. Things that they had been struggling to express, or worse, had felt only they in their isolation thought about, became social, shareable. Speaking of things, of inferiority and ambiguity, or irony and obsession, brought relief, and perhaps for the first time gave the children a sense that there were meaningful human creations that one could discover in a classroom.

Yet not all concepts have been verbalized, and the children frequently talked of having feelings and desires that no words I gave them expressed adequately. They had to create new words, or develop new forms of expression to communicate, and that can neither be taught nor done upon command. We could go to the frontier, however, and speak about the blues, about being bad or hip or cool—about how certain ways of living or historical times created the need for new words. We talked about the nuclear age, the smallness of the modern world, the jargon of democracy and communism, integration and segregation. The children looked in awe at *Finnegans Wake* and Joyce's monumental attempt to forge a new language; they listened to Bob Dylan, recorded the words of soul songs and classical blues, read poetry. We started out talking about words and ended up with life itself. The children opened up and began to display a fearless curiosity about the world.

I sense that I've jumped ahead too quickly, for the whole

thing happened slowly, almost imperceptibly. There were days of despair throughout the whole year, and I never learned how to line the class up at three o'clock. There were days when Alvin was a brilliant inspiring pupil at ten and the most unbearable, uncontrollable nuisance at eleven thirty; when after a good lesson some children would turn angry and hostile, or lose interest in everything. There were small fights and hostilities, adjustments and readjustments in the children's relationships to each other and to me. I had to enlarge my vision as a human being, learn that if the complex and contradictory nature of life is allowed to come forth in the classroom there are times when it will do so with a vengeance.

I still stuck to the curriculum as much as possible. The social studies was impossible so I collected the books and returned them to the bookroom. It was too painful to see the children twist their faces into stupid indifference and hear their pained dull answers accompanied by nervous drumming on the desks.

"New York is a large modern country."

"The Hudson is an important ocean."

"The Industrial Revolution was a benefit to all."

Better drop it altogether, try anything so long as it didn't humiliate the children. These answers were not a function of the children's lack of experience, as the hopelessly respectable anti-poverty program believes; rather they were a direct response to the institutionalized hypocrisy that is characteristic of schools in the United States today.

I brought part of my library to school and temporarily substituted it for social studies. The children were curious about those Greeks and Latins who contributed so many words and concepts to our language. I brought in books on Greek and Roman architecture and art, as well as Robert Graves's version of the *Iliad*, a paperback translation of Apuleius' *Cupid and Psyche*, the *Larousse Encyclopedia of Mythology*, and anything else that seemed relevant or interesting. I showed the books to the children and let them disappear into their desks. It was made clear that the books were to be read, the pages to be turned. If someone reads a book so intensely that the book is bruised it is flattering to the book.

For three-quarters of an hour a day the Pantheon circulated along with Floyd Patterson and J. D. Salinger, Partridge's dictionary of word origins made its way through the class with Langston Hughes and the Bobbsey twins. Anything I could get my hands on was brought to class—a great deal remained unread, and some books I hadn't read myself shocked and surprised the class. They were sexy and popular. Later that

year my supervisor told me I was running a very effective indi-
vidualized reading program. That may have been it, but the
truth seemed simpler and less structured. I overwhelmed the
class with books, many of which I loved, and let them discover for themselves what they liked. There were no reports
to be written, no requirements about numbers of pages to be
read. Some children hardly read at all, others devoured whatever was in the room. The same is true of my friends.

Robert Jackson grabbed a book on Greek architecture,
copied floor plans and perspective drawings, and finally, leaping out of the book, created a reasonably accurate scale model
of the Parthenon. Alvin and Michael built a clay volcano,
asked for and got a chemistry book which showed them how
to simulate an eruption. Sam, Thomas, and Dennis fought
their way through war books; through the Navy, the Seabees,
the Marines, and the Paratroops. The girls started with the
Bobbsey twins and worked through to romantic novels and,
in the case of a few, Thurber and O. Henry. I learned that
there were no books to fear, and having been divested of my
fear of idleness, I also wasn't worried if some children went
through periods of being unable to do anything at all.

People entering my classroom during those forty-five minutes of "social" studies usually experienced an initial sense of
disorder followed by surprise at the relative calm of the room.
If they bothered to look more closely or ask they would find
that most of the children were working.

I remember once a supervisor from the District Office
visited my class in late October. She entered the room un-
announced, said nothing to me, but proceeded to ask the
children what they were doing. In small groups or individually
they showed her. She was pleased until she came to Ralph,
who boldly told her that he was spending the morning ripping
up pieces of paper—which is precisely what he had been doing
all morning. Her whole impression of the classroom changed.
I was a failure, allowing a child not to work, the thought of
it . . . shocking. She took the situation into her own hands
and spoke to Ralph. He merely turned a dumb face to her,
rolled his eyes, and went back to his paper. She left, mutter-
ing something about discipline and emotional disturbance.

Ralph wasn't the only one who couldn't do anything for
a while. When I started bringing books to school and opening
the supply closets to the class, most children demurred from
any change in routine. They wanted the social studies books
even though they learned nothing from them; they enjoyed
copying the mindless exercises that kept them dull and secure
in class. It was just that I, as a teacher, couldn't pretend they

were learning just to make our life together quieter and easier. So, with the textbooks gone many children stuck to chess and checkers. The girls started playing jacks, and with my encouragement created a vocabulary to describe the jack fever that seized them.

For days, until they got bored or became bold enough to explore new books, strange personal books they had never seen before, the girls lived in the throes of jackomania. The jack contagion spread until almost every girl cultivated jackophilia. As a reaction to this the boys in the class became jackophobes and misjackophiles. I managed in this way to keep the children talking about what they were doing, and to push them to explore their actions. Little by little groups of girls formed to read together and talk about books. I remember the stir caused by *Mary Jane*, Dorothy Sterling's book about a Negro girl who helped desegregate a Southern junior high school. I read the class a selection on Mary Jane's first day in the previously all-white school. The demand for the book was so great that I got four copies and let them circulate.

Because the children began choosing their work slowly I could follow the many directions pursued during "social" studies, could sometimes jump ahead, and getting a sense of the children's tastes and preferences, make sure material was there. Also I had time to listen and even participate in some of the projects. Alvin and Michael were joined by Charles, Franklin, and Thomas C. in their volcanic endeavors. After the first successful eruption created by Alvin's mother's vinegar poured over Michael's mother's baking soda, the volcano became less interesting. The five boys sat poring over the book of experiments I gave them, planning and plotting how to steal the equipment.

I asked the assistant principal for equipment for the kids, and he replied that the school hadn't received any. When I told that to the boys they laughed and said they knew where it was, only they'd never see it because their school was in ᴴarlem. I was incredulous, but have since learned how often the children are acutely aware of what the staff attempts to conceal from them. Instead of becoming moralistic and telling the children that they couldn't possibly know about such things as hidden science materials I challenged them and they led me into the hall and up to a locked supply closet. The next day I managed to get the key and found just what I'd been told, several years' untouched, packaged science supplies—batteries in sealed boxes dating as much as five years back, bells, buzzers, chemicals, aquariums, terrariums—enough for a whole elementary school.

It was useless trying to fight the administration over their irresponsibility. I had done that before in another public school in New York City, had been given thoroughly evasive answers, and found myself transferred to Harlem at the end of the year. The principal may have thought that was a deserving punishment for defiance. At any rate it sobered me—I wanted to teach, and after a few months did not want to leave Harlem and the kids. Grade 6-1 had become a part of me. So I learned to keep quiet, keep the door of my classroom shut, and make believe that the class and I functioned in a vacuum, that the school around us didn't exist. It was difficult not to feel the general chaos—to observe the classes without teachers, the children wandering aimlessly, sometimes wantonly through the halls, disrupting classes, intimidating, extorting, yet being courted by the administration: "Please don't make trouble, anything you want, but no trouble." I kept quiet that year anyway, and tried not to make trouble for them either. I wasn't a good enough teacher yet, or confident enough to accuse others of failing with the children when I wasn't sure of my own work. But I had to get that science equipment, so I volunteered to take care of science supplies for the school, mentioning casually that I noticed that there were some in the closet. The principal gave me the closet key with a smile that said, "Anytime you want to do more work, come to me. Who knows what you could find hidden in the other closets. . . ." Then he asked, truly puzzled, "Do you think those children will get anything out of it?"

We had the equipment, and that was the important thing at the moment. The boys went through many experiments, put together elaborate combinations of bells, buzzers, and lights, and contrived a burglar-alarm system for the classroom. They made a fire extinguisher and invisible ink. After a week they were joined by several girls who took over the equipment as the boys broke away to help Robert with the Parthenon. The groups formed and re-formed as projects developed and were abandoned. It was good to see the children, once so wild over a simple game of chess, move freely about the room, exploring socially and intellectually. Still there were moments of doubt and anxiety; it was difficult to see where this classroom of mine was going.

As usual the children led me. I have found one of the most valuable qualities a teacher can have is the ability to perceive and build upon the needs his pupils struggle to articulate through their every reaction. For this he needs antennae and must constantly work upon attuning himself to the ambience of the classroom. To the mastery of observation of children

must be added the more difficult skill of observing his own
effect upon the class, something only partially done at best.
But if the easy guides of a standard curriculum and authori-
tarian stance are to be discarded any clues arising from actual
experience in the classroom are welcome.

I had brought many things from home for the children;
now they brought things for me to learn from. Sam brought
in a Moms Mabley record and from the other children's reaction it was obvious that she was "in." I had never heard
of her and asked the class who she was. They all volunteered
information: that she was ancient, funny, and nice, that she
liked young boys and kids, that people lined up on 125th Street
whenever she was at the Apollo Theater, that she sounded on
people in the audience.

Sam shyly suggested that we listen to the record instead
of doing reading, and I reluctantly agreed. It was still difficult
for me to discard my schedule with confidence. There was
another problem—I explained to the class that there was no
phonograph in the room or, as far as I knew, in the school.

Thomas S. and Dennis jumped up, asked me to write a
note saying I wanted to borrow a record player, and disappeared with the note, only to reappear in five minutes with
a machine. They knew the exact distribution of all the hidden
and hoarded supplies in the school, and I learned to trust their
knowledge over official statements of what was available.

We listened to Moms, the class explaining the jokes, translating some of her dialect for me. It pleased them to be listened to. After that we kept a phonograph in the room, and
the children brought in the latest records. We listened to them
together at the end of the morning or the afternoon. I tran-
scribed the words and every once in a while put them on the
blackboard and discussed what the songs were all about. One
particularly interesting song was "Do You Love Me?" by
Barry Gordy, Jr.

> You broke my heart because I couldn't dance
> You didn't even want me around.
> And now I'm back to let you know
> I can really shake 'em down.
>
> Do you love me? I can really move.
> Do you love me? I'm in the groove.
> Do you love me? Do you love me
> Now that I can dance?*

* © 1962 Jobete Music Company, Inc. Quoted by permission.

I asked the kids if it really was that important to be able to dance. They replied in veiled terms that I couldn't understand. I pushed them. Why couldn't I understand? Dancing is a simple social phenomenon, it has to do with parties and popularity, not the soul. . . .

That hit something direct. One of the boys said, just loud enough for me to hear, that dancing *was* a soul thing. Others took up the argument, it was a way of being together, of expressing yourself when you were alone, of feeling strong when everything was wrong, of feeling alive in a dead world.

"Besides, Mr. Kohl, they don't only mean dancing. That's a way of saying you can't do nothing, that you're weak. Dancing is kind of, you know, like a symbol."

Alvin explained it to me. It was only a step from there to letting the kids actually dance in class. I started on Friday afternoons, and later let the kids dance when the afternoon work was done. At first only the girls were interested. Half of them would dance (it was The Wobble at that time), while the others would read or talk, or even begin their homework. The boys would hover about the dancers, joking, moving ever so slightly with the music, pushing Michael and Maurice into the Wobble line, urging them to continue the satire of the girls' movement that they were performing in a corner. Once in a while everyone danced—I even tried to overcome my leaden-footed self-consciousness and take a few steps, but my soul wasn't free enough.

Music became an integral part of the classroom. The children brought in their records; I responded with my own. One morning I put twenty-five records ranging from blues and Fats Waller through Thelonious Monk and Coltrane to Mozart and Beethoven on top of the phonograph. During the morning breaks the kids explored freely, and when the music began to interest some individuals enough, I brought in biographies of the composers, pictures of the musicians. We talked in small groups during social studies of chain gangs, field music, modern jazz, rock and roll, child prodigies, anything that came up. A dialogue between the children and myself was developing.

It deepened quickly. Alvin and Ralph decided to wait for me at eight o'clock and spend an hour in the classroom before the class arrived. They were soon joined by Maurice, Michael, Reginald, Pamela, and Brenda W. At one time or another during the year every child went through a phase of coming early. The only limitations I had to impose on this were forced upon me by other teachers who didn't want to be bothered by children so early in the morning and complained to the administration.

I would arrive at the school at eight. Several of the children would be waiting and we would walk the five flights up to the room. One of the boys would take my briefcase, another the keys. Once in the room the children went their own ways. Maurice and Michael went to the phonograph, Alvin to his latest project with Robert Jackson. The girls would play jacks or wash the boards. Grace explored the books on my desk. Every once in a while one of the children would come up to my desk and ask a question or tell me something. The room warmed up to the children, got ready for the day. At first the questions were simple, irrelevant.

"Mr. Kohl, what's today's date?"

"Where is Charles this morning?"

Then there was some testing.

"Mr. Kohl, when are you going to be absent?"

"Will you come back here next year?"

By the end of October a few children were coming to my desk in the morning and saying things that nothing in my life prepared me to understand or respond to.

"Mr. Kohl, the junkies had a fight last night. They cut this girl up bad."

"Mr. Kohl, I couldn't sleep last night, they was shouting and screaming until four o'clock."

"I don't go down to the streets to play, it's not safe."

"Mr. Kohl, those cops are no good. They beat up on this kid for nothing last night."

I listened, hurt, bruised by the harshness of the children's world. There was no response, no indignation or anger of mine, commensurate to what the children felt. Besides, it was relief they wanted, pronouncement of the truth, acceptance of it in a classroom which had become important to them. I could do nothing about the facts, therefore my words were useless. But through listening, the facts remained open and therefore placed school in the context of the children's real world.

At eight o'clock on October 22, Alvin pushed Ralph up to my desk. Ralph handed me "The Rob-Killing of Liebowitz," and retreated.

Last night on 17 St. Liebowitz collected the rent. They told him not to come himself but he came for many years. The junkies got him last night. He wouldn't give them the money so they shot him and took it. They was cops and people runny all over roofs and the streets.

There were people from the news and an ambulance took Liebowitz.

I read Ralph's article to the class and asked them if it were true. There was an awkward silence, then Neomia said with bitterness:

"If you don't believe it you can look in the *Daily News*."

"Mr. Kohl, you don't know what it's like around here."

The others agreed, but when I pressed the class to tell me, silence returned. The more I tried to get the class to talk the dumber the children acted, until they finally denied that there was any truth in Robert's article whatever. The topic was too charged for public discussion; it somehow had to be made private, between each individual child and myself. After all, not everybody saw the same things, and worse perhaps, if things were so bad it would be natural for some of the children to be afraid. So I asked the class to write, as homework in the privacy of their apartments, and tell me what their block was like, what they felt about it. The papers were not to be marked or shown to anybody else in the class. If anybody objected, he didn't have to do the assignment. This was probably the first time in their school lives that the children wrote to communicate, and the first sense they had of the possibilities of their own writing.

The next evening I read the responses.

*Neomia*                           WHAT A BLOCK!

My block is the most terrible block I've ever seen. There are at lease 25 or 30 narcartic people in my block. The cops come around there and tries to act bad but I bet inside of them they are as scared as can be. They even had in the papers that this block is the worst block, not in Manhattan but in New York City. In the summer they don't do nothing except shooting, stabbing and fighting. They hang all over the stoops and when you say excuse me to them they hear you but they just don't feel like moving. Some times they make me so mad that I feel like slaping them and stuffing and bag of garbage down their throats. Theres only one policeman who can handle these people and we all call him "Sunny." When he come around in his cop car the people run around the corners, and he wont let anyone sit on the stoops. If you don't believe this story come around some time and you'll find out.

*Marie*

My block is the worse block you ever saw people getting killed or stabbed men and women in building's taking dope.

And when the police come around the block the block be so clean that nobody will get hurt. There's especially one police you even beat woman you can't even stand on your own stoop he'll chase you off. And sometimes the patrol wagon comes around and pick up al the dope addicts and one day they picked up this man and when his wife saw him and when she went to tell the police that that's her husband they just left so she went to the police station and they let him go. You can never trust anyone around my block you even get robbed when the children in my building ask me to come down stairs I say no because you don't know what would happen. Only sometimes I come down stairs not all the time.

*Sonia*            THE STORY ABOUT MY BLOCK

My block is dirty and it smell terrible
The children picks fights. And it hardly have room to play. its not a very long thing to write about, but if you were living there you won't want to stay there no longer. it have doopedics and gabbage pan is spill on the side walk and food is on the ground not everyday but sometimes children make fire in the backyard. on the stoop is dirty. I go out to play that the End about My block.

*Phyllis*                    MY BLOCK

My block has a lot of kids who thing that the can beat everybody (like a lot of blocks) They pick on children that they know they can beat. There trouble makers and blabbers mouths.

*Charisse*                    MY BLOCK

I live 62 E 120st My neighborhood is not so bad. Everyone has children in the block. Many of the children are Spanish. Some of them run around nude and dirty. Some of the house are so dirty you would be sacre to come in the door. Sometime the drunks come out and fight. Some of the house are nice and clean. The block is not to dirty its the people inside of it. At night it's very quite. But if you come in my building at about 10:00 you would be surprise to see some naked children running around like animals. The mothers don't even seem to care about them. Many of the children ages run

from 1 to 4 years of age. Many of the people in the block
drink so much they don't have time for the children. The
children have no place to play they have the park but the
parents don't care enough to take them. Now you have a
idea of what my block is like.

*Ralph*          MY NEIGHBORHOOD

I live on 117 street, between Madison and 5th avenue.
All the bums live around here. But the truth is they don't live
here they just hang around the street. All the kids call it
"Junky's Paradise." Because there is no cops to stop them.
I wish that the cops would come around and put all the bums
out of the block and put them in jail all their life. I would
really like it very much if they would improve my neighborhood. I don't even go outside to play because of them. I just
play at the center or someplace else.

*Gail*          MY BLOCK

My block is sometimes noisy and sometimes quiet when
its noisy children and grownups are out side listening to the
boys playing the steel drums or there's a boy who got hit by
a car or something. When the block is quiet, there is a storm,
raining or snowing and people don't come out side. Farther
down the block near Park Avenue, some of the houses are
not kept clean.
There's a lot right next to a building and there's a lot of
trash, you can see rats running back and forth. The Sanitation
Department cleans it every week, but it just gets dirty again
because people throw garbage out the windows. From Madison
Ave. to about the middle of the block the houses are kept
clean. The back yards are keep swept and the stoops are clean.
I like my building and block.

*Carol*

Around my block all you can see is drug addits. The
other day the Cops came and took over 15 men in the cops
wagon and they came out the next day but one man shim they
kept him beated him from 7 in the morning until 1:30 in the
afternoon because they thought he had something to do with
the Rob Killing of Lebrowize.

*Ronnie*

I think my block is not as lively as it use to be cause all the jive time people are moving out. I think my block is nice compare tó 117 St were people be getting kill.

*Charles*

My block is a dirty crumby block.

*Thomas S.*

Ounce their was a gang fight around my block and the police came and a man got shot. And their was detives around my block and junkies shot at a copes and a lady curse out the copes and they broke in a lady house. Around 119 street a cop was bricked and kill and junkies took dop and needies.

*Kathleen*                                    ABOUT MY BLOCK

Around my block theirs no trees on the side walks like the Park on the outside but of course theres not going to be any trees on the side walks but there are some trees on the side walks mabe in brooklyn or long island. New Jersey and Queens but I know there are some in long island I know that because thats like a little country in some parts of it. And around my block I have nice friends and nice neighbors of my mother, people are nice around my block I go to Church with my friends and we all go together and learn more and more about God and I like it very much Because when I grow up to be a lady (if I live to see and if gods willing) and know all about God and understand the facts I want to be a nice mannered lady and go to church as long as I live to see.

The day after we talked about them. I had asked for the truth, and it presented its ugly head in the classroom, yet I didn't know what to do about it. That was all I could say to the children—that I was moved, angry, yet as powerless to change things as they were. I remembered How We Became Modern America, the books I couldn't use, and felt dumb, expressionless—how else can one put up with such lies of progress, prosperity, and cheerful cooperation when we do face problems. The next day the children wrote of how they would change things if they could.

### *Thomas S.*   IF I COULD CHANGE MY BLOCK

If I could change my block, I would first get read of all
of the wine heads and clean up the gobash and then try to
improve the buildings and paint the apartments. That's what
I would do.

### *Neomia*

If I could change my block I would stand on Madison
Ave and throw nothing but Teargas in it. I would have all the
people I liked to get out of the block and then I would become
very tall and have big hands and with my big hands I would
take all of the narcartic people and pick them up with my
hand and throw them in the nearest river and Oceans. I would
go to some of those old smart alic cops and throw them in the
Oceans and Rivers too. I would let the people I like move into
the projects so they could tell their friends that they live in
a decent block. If I could do this you would never see 117 st
again.

### *Kathleen*                    MY BLOCK

If I could change my block I would have new house but
in it I would have all the bums take out of it. There would be
garden where I live. There would be some white people live
there we would have all colors not just Negro. There would
be 7 room apt. There be low rent for the poor family. The
poor family would have the same thing as the average or rich
family have. There would be club for the boys and girls. There
would be place where the Old could come. Where the young
can share there problem

### *Brenda T.*

If I could change my block I would put all the bums on
an Island where they can work there. I would give them lots
of food. But I wouldn't let no whiskey be brought to them.
After a year I would ship them to new York and make them
clean up junk in these back yard and make them maybe make
a baseball diamond and put swings basketball courts etc. When
I get thought they'll never want whiskey or dope cause If I
catch them I'll make a them work day and night with little
food. Lunch would be at 5:00 super 10:00 bed 1:00 (If caught
2 times) breakfast 8:30. Get up at 3.00

*Marie*    HOW I WOULD CHANGE MY BLOCK

If I could change my block I would take out all of the junkies and I would take out all of the old buildings and put in new ones and give hot water every day and make a play street out of my block.

That's what I would do if I could

*Thomas C.*

Well I would like to change my block into a play street, first I'd take all the junkies out the block and take the parking cars out the block and make whaw that everyman put their cars in a garage at nights. Because too many children get hit by cars and make all the buildings neat and clean with stream and hot and cold water.

*Anastasia*

The very first thing that I would like to do to change my block if I could, put up a no litering sign to keep away stange people who hang around the steps. Nexs I would have less garbage containers on the sidewalks, expecially those that are uncovered because they are unsightly and unhealthy, and last bus at least. I would make a carfew at least 5 p.m. for ander age children to be upt the corners, sidewalks, and if they are not, hold their parents severly responsible for any harm that befails them.

*Charles*

If I could do anything to chang my block tear down the buildings on both sides. And have a school on one side and a center on the other. Inside the center there would be a swimming pool inside and also a gym. And outside a softball field and also four baskball courts.

*Sonia*

if I could of change my block I would make it cleaner no gabbage pans open and falling down and not so many fights and don't let it have dead animals in the street.

How we became modern America, how we became modern man—that was our problem, my problem to teach, but where to start, at what moment in history does one say, "Ah, here's where it all began"? How could the children get some saving perspective on the mad chaotic world they existed in, some sense of the universality of struggle, the possibility of revolution and change, and the strength to persist? That, if anything, was my challenge as a teacher—it was spelled out before me unambiguously. Could I find anything in human history and the human soul that would strengthen the children and save them from despair?

I had reached this point by the end of October, a few days before Halloween.

Halloween in Harlem is frightening and exciting. I remained at school until four o'clock that afternoon cleaning the classroom and thinking. Things seemed painfully slow, the children distant. Darkness seemed to be setting in everywhere; maybe it was the coming of winter, I don't know, but I was on the verge of tears. Another beautiful morning, then a chaotic hostile afternoon. My energy disappeared and at that moment it didn't seem possible to continue all the way to June. The silence of the room comforted me, however. I walked about picking up papers, looking at the desk tops and scratches: "Alvin is a chipmunk," "Michael's mother's best friend is a roach," "Margie likes Carol"—it was good to discover such underground vitality in the class. The children's confounding contradictory presence was still there. I found myself smiling, thinking of the next day, of my fiftieth new beginning of the year. Things didn't seem so bad. I wanted to be home planning and preparing for the next day, packed my books, and left.

The street was something else. Painted creatures streaking up and down, stockings full of flour crashing on heads, chests, missiles descending from rooftops, wild laughter, children fighting, tumbling over a world they owned for half a day.

I remembered my own sedate Halloweens—planned trick-or-treating and plastic masks. Suddenly Sylvia ran up, threatened me with a stocking. I fumbled for a quarter which she threw to some little children. They dove for it as she bumped me and ran off. Someone else chalked my coat—it was Michael, or maybe Maurice—I moved as quickly as possible to the bus stop, changed my mind and took a cab home. My heart was pounding; the wildness frightened me. But by the time the cab reached 90th Street I was jealous. No mask or ritual occasion had ever set me free.

After dinner I had to be on the streets again. It was five

flights down. I reached the landing of the second floor lost in a fantasy of Harlem Halloweens. There were people talking on the ground floor, a couple saying good night to someone who had moved in, a female face. I realized how lonely I was; wanted to wait until the couple had left and then trick-or-treat myself.

They left, the door was closed and I stared at it, paused, then decided that if a light was still on after I had a beer I would knock. I returned after six beers and it was on. To be true to the children and myself, I knocked. That was how I met Judy, my wife.

We talked well into the night, two months of days with 6-1 poured out of me, the anguish and the hope, my own uncertainty and my confidence. All of the contradictions that lived in my classroom were articulated for the first time. I showed her the children's writing, the ridiculous textbooks I had to use. Then, after it had all tumbled out, I could look at her and try to discover who she was.

We talked of college, Harvard and Chatham, of how distant it seemed. We had both been to Europe; she had just returned though I had been back for several years. I remembered that once an academic career in philosophy seemed all that was open to me; remembered dreading spending my life at a university, reading, pretending to be interested in what I was doing. Judy talked of herself. I don't remember exactly what she said—at that moment in my life I felt the strength to fall in love, and though it happened more slowly than that, a life for the two of us began that Halloween. I was momentarily freed of my obsession with school, and when, after we parted that night, I thought about the children, it was with a freshness I hadn't known for weeks. Things began to fit together; it gradually became clear what had to be taught the children.

There was no other place to start than at the beginning, before so-called civilized man had already built decay into his "eternal" works. We had to begin with man just emerging as Homo sapiens, and with the growth of civilization in its birthplaces—Africa and Asia. Since I had to teach the children I had to learn myself. My education, like most in the West, went no further back than Greece. Egypt, Mesopotamia, India, China—thousands of years earlier, yet no less sophisticated or, it may turn out, significant to the history of modern man, were ignored. History for years has been arbitrarily limited in schools in the United States to European and post-Columbian American history. This gives one a false perspective on the development of man, one precariously close to a white perspective.

That year I did a lot of probing and research, tracing
Greek myths to earlier African and Asiatic sources, discovering the wonders of Sumer and Akkad, of the early Indian kingdoms and the Egyptian dynasties. As this whole new world
opened for me I shared it with the children in class. Other
teachers thought there was something ludicrous in researching
to teach at an elementary level. They advised me to find a text
and keep one lesson ahead.

The one-lesson-ahead morality is what makes so many
elementary school classes dull and uninspiring. The teacher
doesn't understand much of what he is teaching, and worse,
doesn't care that he doesn't understand. How can the children
be expected to be alert, curious, and excited when the teacher
is so often bored?

The need for elementary teachers who are serious-
thinking adults, who explore and learn while they teach, who
know that to teach young children mathematics, history, or
literature isn't to empty these subjetcs of content or complexity but to reduce and present them in forms which are accurate, honest, and open to development and discovery, and
therefore require subtle understanding and careful work, cannot be exaggerated. The time has passed when the school-
marm, equipped to teach the three R's by rote and impose
morality by authority, has something useful and important to
give children.

As I learned early history, there was a text for the class
that did make my work easier. Through some ironic chance,
P.S. 103, with no complete set of arithmetic books and barely
enough American history books, did have one set of forty-five
new social studies books that started with the "cave man" and
went through to modern man. Copies of the book were spread
throughout the fifth and sixth grades, three or four per room,
as part of the miscellaneous collection of obsolete or irrelevant
textbooks that passed for class libraries. Once again, making
judicious use of Thomas and Dennis, I managed to piece
together the full set of books for my class.

As a framework around which to build a history of man's
social and cultural life the book wasn't bad, yet it was so vast
and ambitious—the entire history of mankind in two hundred
illustrated pages. I had to select and elaborate, create a focus
and perspective for the class. I also had to let them know it
was *my* focus and that there were any number of other ways
to look at the same events and facts. One could look at
"progress," at artistic creativity, invention, power . . . I wanted
to look at the internal and external conditions of human existence that gave rise to human inequalities, at the attempts that

have been made to rectify them and the degree to which certain inequalities may be inevitable. I wanted the children to see themselves in the perspective of history, to know the changes of fortune, of the balance of wealth and power, that have constituted history, and of the equally real change of the oppressed into the oppressor. I wanted them to be able to persist, revolt, and change things in our society and yet not lose their souls in the process.

It was the most romantic and idealistic thing I ever attempted and the one I believed in the most. I am not so idealistic or romantic now. My recollections of 6-1 are tinged with bitterness and too clear knowledge of the present and what I failed to give the children, what I couldn't give them. Yet the effort was worth it. Robert Jackson and Alvin remember what we learned, however remote it is from their present lives; other kids remember too, Michael and Ralph, Dennis, Pamela and Grace, the ones I've spoken to recently. They remember, but that year, only four years ago, is remote. In the excitement of living through that year I forgot what a short time a year is in a lifetime of trouble.

That's now another story. Four years ago I worried about the textbook. It presented history as an increasingly successful and thoroughly inevitable movement toward the present and expressed a hopelessly dated and unrealistic faith in "history's" capacity to solve human problems satisfactorily. Events and cultures were "important" only as they related to the successes of mid-twentieth century America (meaning the United States of America and blithely omitting Canada and Latin America). In the book there was no sense of uncertainty or indecision, of the complexity of understanding historical events and the shifting perspective of the present. Its every page seemed to say, We are over the hump, things are fine, we are rational. There was no humility or depth in its pages—it presented Greece without slaves or passion, all Apollo, no Dionysus; Rome without debauch or greed; industrial and urban society without exploitation or slums. The children were firmly expected to learn that the way the book presented history was *the* way it had happened. There was but one way the past could be viewed and that was as a moralistic justification of our present life. In a world of rapidly changing perspectives this is a hopeless and dangerous way to teach history.

For my class it was even more perilous, for if to the United States' two hundred years was added the rest of the history of mankind to justify the misery and oppression the children experienced, the inevitability of their situation and the hypocrisy of "history" would only be more fully confirmed.

I had to create out of the material in the book a vision of history totally at variance with the book's orientation. It was essential for the children to learn of change and of the needs of the powerful to believe the present eternal. They had to see that one man's "barbarian" was another's "civilized" ideal, one nation's hero another's villain. They had to learn how uneasy and difficult any marriage of history and morals has to be.

Despite all this, the new text was much better than the other ones on modern America. It started with man wandering the earth, hunting, loving, and fighting to survive. The children knew about these conditions, could readily imagine the earliest state of man without being threatened by lies and hypocrisy. What they needed in order to open them up was just such a start without presuppositions. For the first few weeks of this new social studies we talked of the phenomenology of early man—what his experiences might have been, how he may have reacted and felt. We talked of families and loyalties and conflicts, of bands and tribes and the formation of larger human groups. We spoke of the division of work and the selection of leaders, and of the additional factors introduced into life by existence in larger groups of individuals. Then we spoke of what man *might* become, and the range of possibilities open to him.

It was natural to consider the world man lived in as well and discuss the resources and limitations it presented. The children became curious about the earth, and I got a physical globe which provided hours of fascinated watching for some of the class. There were no national boundaries on the globe, no cities or states. The rivers, mountains, oceans were not named. Blue, green, and brown mutely signified water and land, high and low. I wanted the children to imagine an ahistorical earth. Later we traced the changing boundaries of man's states and nations on the globe. The children saw the many different things that happened simultaneously on earth and we talked of the preselection of a small fragment of them that constituted the "history" their text presented.

Once, later in the year, I adopted a suggestion Michel Butor implied in his novel *Degrees* and developed a social studies unit on what occurred in the world during the year 1492, the year our class text said a "new" world was "discovered." The class developed a unit in horizontal history, studying the pre-Columbian civilization of the Americas as well as Columbus' voyage. We also discussed the expulsion of the Jews and Moors from Spain and their dispersal over Europe and North Africa. The kingdoms of Africa were discussed, as well as events in India, China, Japan, and Melanesia. Then we discussed historical "importance" and the need to talk of "importance for whom, at what historical moment, for what purpose."

To create a unit like this a teacher has a lot of work to do. There are no textbooks that do the work for you—the sources must be sought, time must be spent on research and planning. No education courses help, one must create the unit out of one's own knowledge and understanding, and must acquire this knowledgs and understanding through hard intellectual work. It is no less true, though perhaps less obvious, that the same work must be done even when one has a textbook. Keeping one lesson ahead of the children is worthless. One must be more than one lesson ahead of the book to explain things to young children and help them understand that their doubts and questions, the things that take them beyond the textbook, are the very essence of learning.

While teaching about early man, I read history, anthropology, archeology, art criticism; brought in books and pictures and maps for the children, and in trying to answer their questions found myself looking into things as diverse as the domestication of animals, cave painting, stone implements, and early technology. The children began to look too, wanted increasingly to answer questions for themselves. Some of them began discovering encyclopedias and the library—things they had been subjected to before but that had previously made no sense to them. Because they saw me researching they learned to do research. They wouldn't have learned had I merely told them to do it.

The class moved from earliest man through to the first settlements in Egypt and Mesopotamia, discussing conditions for the creation of cities and states, the need for water and the selection of river valley sites, the advantages and disadvantages of large cities and states, the problems of labor and authority . . . one thing led to another as the children probed into life in the earliest cities. In a way Sumer became a model the children used to help them understand the complex and often cruel ways of modern cities. We discussed the distribution of wealth, specialization of labor, and the creation of inequalities within Mesopotamian and Egyptian society, contrasting the two and trying to understand something of stability and change in human affairs. The children discovered the need for writing just as the Mesopotamians and Egyptians did, and in listening to the myths of these societies, we heard the people speaking of themselves, of their expectations and sufferings, their heroes and villains. At this point the Social

Studies and Reading joined with the Vocabulary to give the class a picture of man the creator struggling, even at the beginning of his recorded history, with his own imperfect social and moral creations.

IN THOSE DAYS I was still in love with Harvard. Being there as an undergraduate had meant an opening of life to me, not so much a denial of the Bronx where I grew up as an involvement in worlds I never conceived existed. I learned about art, literature, and philosophy, and during my college years wanted to be an academician myself, to teach philosophy at a university and be a scholar. I even spent several years at graduate school as a Ph.D. candidate in philosophy before discovering that for all my love of scholarship I was too restless to be a good scholar. I preferred the challenge of human beings to that of books and loved teaching for what it could offer humanly. I didn't want to teach philosophy as a subject and was most involved when working with children and helping them to come into closer contact with themselves, as my better teachers had helped me. Still, I was grateful for my years at Harvard and wanted to introduce my pupils to an institution that had once been valuable to me and that could in the future be important to some of them.

So, one day in November I invited the children in 6-1 to take a trip to Cambridge with Judy and me. That was the first the children had heard of Judy and they were more interested in her relationship to me than the trip. I told the class how we had met but little else. When I returned to the idea of the trip only ten children were interested.

On the morning of the trip, only six showed up. Alvin and his mother were waiting in front of the school when Judy drove up in her VW, a minute after I arrived in my Ford Falcon. It was seven thirty Saturday morning, and though Alvin was prancing excitedly about, his mother seemed cold and tired. It was unfair to drag her from a Saturday-morning sleep. She had seven children to send to school every weekday morning. Yet she had to come to meet us, for her sake and because Alvin insisted. After a few casual words she returned home and Alvin went over to Judy. They started chatting and I looked, astonished, at the transformation. Alvin, wild in class, often brilliant but equally often scared and unresponsive, was perfectly charming and in control of the situation away from school. He seemed another, happier and more relaxed child. I remember wondering what school could possibly have done to him.

Pamela and Grace arrived together with their mothers.

The contrast between the two women was no less striking than the contrast between their daughters. Mrs. Brown, Grace's mother, was a tall forceful West Indian. A closer look revealed the extraordinary intelligence that Grace displayed the moment she entered school, a thin nervous child who could read in kindergarten as well as most of the other children read in the fifth grade. On the other hand Mrs. Reed seemed so young, fragile, and resigned. Pamela was as pretty as her mother was handsome, and she too seemed fragile. My judgment has never been so wrong, for Pamela and her mother, too, have the kind of internal strength that makes an external demonstration unnecessary. Later that year I lost my temper and turned my anger on Pamela. Never in my life has a person looked back at me so thoroughly unconvinced of guilt and so free of paranoia as Pamela did that day. I confronted myself in her eyes and fell silent in class. I was wrong and foolish and could do no less than apologize.

After Mrs. Reed and Mrs. Brown left, Dianne appeared unexpectedly. She had not shown any interest in coming during the week, but she had set her hair, put on her best dress, and somehow talked Maurice into carrying her mother's fancy (and half-empty) suitcase to the cars. He had said that he was coming so many times during the week that I didn't believe he meant it.

We waited for other children to arrive, Maurice and Alvin talking to Judy, the girls shyly approaching me. At eight thirty we decided that the three girls would travel with me and the two boys with Judy. There was no point waiting any longer.

We got into the cars and I was ready to start off when Alvin spied Robert Jackson peeking around the corner of 118th Street. He was squinting through his glasses, looking toward our cars, but unable to approach. Alvin opened the door and was next to Robert in a minute; then dragged him toward Judy's car, joking, talking, pushing, until Robert was in the back seat next to Maurice, and Alvin said casually: "It doesn't matter if Robert doesn't have a suitcase or pajamas. Harvard isn't far away."

We reached Cambridge at three in the afternoon and checked into the Brattle Inn. I took one suite of rooms for the boys and myself, and Judy took another one across the hall for the girls. There was still time to visit the Fogg Art Museum, to tour the houses and meet some of my friends and classmates who were now instructors and assistant professors. I wanted to show off Widener Library, the university museum, and Harvard Yard to the children and share in their first impressions of a great university. Judy and I let the children settle into their rooms and went out for an hour to have a drink and relax. We agreed to pick the children up at four o'clock and tour the university. When we arrived at the girls' rooms, Pamela, Grace, and Dianne were on the rug in the sitting room playing jacks. Across the hall Robert was drawing, Alvin reading, and Maurice watching television. Everyone but Robert was in pajamas. They had reached their destination—individual beds, clean rooms, space, and quiet. They didn't want to see a university if it meant leaving the Brattle Inn.

We never did see much of Harvard. The children had dinner in that night and begged Judy and me to go out and leave them. They spread themselves through the rooms of the two suites, savoring the luxury of space and quiet they had never known before. The university was too remote and abstract; it was what I offered the children in ignorance of their needs. We returned to New York on Sunday, and when I returned to class on Monday I understood better how much there was for me to learn from the children about the realities of their lives.

At the same time things were happening in class. Robert Jackson the artist, the terrifyingly silent boy, began to emerge. He listened avidly to the myths of Egypt and Mesopotamia, and made his own study of Greece and Rome. I was keenly aware of his attention. Robert never spoke voluntarily and for a long time refused to answer any questions. Alvin and Ralph were his emissaries to me, and only through them did I receive occasional communication from him. However, he always turned in homework, and did more than was required. In corners of the neatly written sheet were illustrations and illuminations. At the bottom of the page Robert added work he made up himself. I could sense he was hungry.

Then came vocabulary and our study of human origins. Robert actually volunteered answers and questions, displayed a mature grasp of the material and an alert subtle mind. He responded during these hours as if a whole world were opening up before him. But that was still the limit. As the subject changed or the class had free time Robert withdrew into silence. He drew, not voluntarily, but mostly at the command of other children. He read books but gave them up easily if another child even expressed mild interest in them. Slowly he managed to go through some of the books on Greece and Rome, but he never had them long enough. It was no good my trying to protect his rights; he then avoided things altogether.

I was distressed by Robert's passivity and was at a loss to help him. One day I brought an orange cardboard binder filled

with loose-leaf paper to school. It was for my observations on
the vocabulary lessons. During free time that morning I became exasperated by the ease with which Robert yielded a
book to Margie, who merely glanced at it and stuffed it in her
desk. I wanted to say something to him, yet words were useless, would only cause further withdrawal. *Maybe I could give
him something that he wouldn't surrender so easily* . . . the
only thing on my desk was the notebook. An idea cautiously
formed; I took the notebook to Robert and said that his
interests in myths and history was so obvious, and his grasp
of the discussions in class so full that I felt he might want to
go beyond reading books and write and illustrate one himself.
    He looked at me as if I were mad.
    "Me?"
    "Why not you? Somebody writes books; anyone can try.
That's the only way to discover how well you can do. Why
don't you take this notebook and try. You don't have to show
me or anybody else what you do if you don't want."
    A sly triumphant look came over Robert's face as he
snatched the notebook out of my hand. I retreated to my desk,
afraid of spoiling the whole thing with unnecessary words.
    It wasn't until a week later that I discovered that my
attempt had worked. Maurice came up to my desk before class
and asked me if Robert was the only one in class who could
write a book. I said no and then Maurice asked me what
Robert was writing about anyway. Robert, it seems, refused
to tell him or even show him one page.
    I explained that I didn't know either, and that Robert
could be writing about anything, that the book was private
unless he chose to show it to anybody, and that included me.
    "What about me? Could I write a book?—even about
myself, the truth, you know . . ."
    "It's been done before. There's no reason why you can't
do it."
    I promised to bring Maurice a binder (having the symbol
of being sanctioned to write privately and as one pleased was
very important) and the next morning brought a dozen to
school. I explained to the entire class that some children
wanted to write their own books and that the binders were
available for anybody who cared to write. I also explained
that though I was available to help or to read their work for
pleasure, still the books were their private property—the
author's control over his work would be respected completely.
There was no mention of grading or grammar as it never
occurred to me then even to bother with a disclaimer.
    The children were suspicious of my talk about privacy

and wanted to know what kinds of things people write books about. Though they had seen some of the scope of literature in the books I brought to class, I think the children still believed there were only two kinds of books—the "good" books they read in school which were nice, boring, and unreal, and the "bad" books they sneaked to each other which were filthy, exciting, and unreal. It was hard to explain what people wrote about. Instead of trying I spent the next week selecting from my library and reading to the children, asking them to attend to the subject and to the writer's voice as well. I read about love, hate, jealousy, fear; of war and religion, quest and loss. I read in voices that were ironic, cynical, joyous, and indifferent. The class and I talked of the writer's selection of his subject and the development of his voice; of the excitement of not knowing entirely where the book you set out to write will take you.

A few children dared at first, then more, until finally most of the children in the class attempted some written exploration. I put an assignment on the board before the children arrived in the morning and gave the class the choice of reading, writing, or doing what was on the board. At no time did any child have to write, and whenever possible I let the children write for as long as their momentum carried them. Time increasingly became the servant of substance in the classroom. At the beginning of the semester I had tried to use blocks of time in a predetermined, preplanned way—first reading, then social studies, arithmetic, and so forth. Then I broke the blocks by allowing free periods. This became confining and so I allowed the length of periods to vary according to the children's and my interest and concentration. Finally we reached a point where the class could pursue things without the burden of a required amount of work that had to be passed through every day. This meant that there were many things that the class didn't "cover"; that there were days without arithmetic and weeks without spelling or my dear "vocabulary." Many exciting and important things were missed as well as many dull things. But the children learned to explore and invent, to become obsessed by things that interested them and follow them through libraries and books back into life; they learned to believe in their own curiosity and value the intellectual and literary, perhaps even in a small way the human, quest without being overly burdened with a premature concern for results.

I remembered my student teaching when I watched the children in 6-1 writing. It was in a middle-class white school, well run and quiet almost to the point of terror. My student teaching had consisted mostly in giving remedial reading lessons to "difficult" children, *i.e.*, the two Negroes and ten Puerto Ricans in the school. I soon learned that the teachers' tyranny over their "white" pupils was so complete and their fear of the "nonwhites" so great that they did anything to keep the "nonwhites," especially the boys, out of the classrooms. They created unnecessary monitorships and perpetual errands for these poor harassed children, and then blamed the children for being reading problems.

One of my "problem" students turned out to be interested in architecture, and the two of us had been exploring the floor plans of Chartres Cathedral together. One day my supervisor was absent and I was allowed to take over the class. That morning Stanley spent two and a half hours putting the plan of Chartres on the blackboard. I brought in slides and pictures, and for most of the morning tried to show the class what went into the building of a cathedral. They had been studying technology so superficially that I wanted them to understand how problems arose and were solved—and for a change I wanted to show them something beautiful in school.

The morning had seemed to go well, only I was surprised to see a little committee waiting for me after class. There were five children looking nervous and distressed, their faces grave and serious. The spokesman stepped forward and cleared his throat.

"Mr. Kohl, there is something that distresses us. We spent this morning looking at that cathedral. It was very beautiful but, Mr. Kohl, will it help us? There is so much that has to be done, we have no time to waste, my father would be very upset. How will it get us into college?"

Fifth grade, "no time to waste"—I thought of those poor unsmiling children at such a "good" school and of my thirty-six children, writing, not rushing, taking the time to explore.

Not that some of the children in 6-1 weren't initially distressed by the freedom of the room and the increasingly experimental curriculum. They were and told me, and at times I almost wavered and returned to the crutches of standard preplanned material. But I believed in what was happening in class and bore the uncertainty and days of chaos until together we saw work emerge that none of us expected or believed possible.

Maurice was the first to show me his book.

# THE STORY OF MY LIFE

## FOREWORD

This story is about a boy named Maurice and his life as
it is and how it will be. Maurice is in the six grade now but
this story will tell about his past, present, and future. It will
tell you how he lived and how he liked it or disliked it. It will
tell you how important he was and happy or sad he was in this
world it will tell you all his thoughts. It may be pleasant and
it may be horrible in place but what ever it is it will be good
and exciting but! their will be horrible parts. This story will be
made simple and easy but in places hard to understand. This
is a nonfiction book.

## WHERE I WAS BORN

In all story they beat around the bush before they tell you
the story well I am not this story takes place in the Metropolitan Hospitle.

When I was born I couldn't see at first. but like all families my father was waiting outside after a hour or so I could
see shadows. The hospital was very large and their were millions of beds and plenty of people. And their were people in
chairs rolling around, people in beds, and people walking
around with trays with food or medicine on it. Their was
people rolling people in bed and there were people bleeding
crying yelling or praying I was put at a window with other
babies so my father could see me their was a big glass and
lots of people around me so I could see a lot of black shapes.
And since I was a baby I tried to go through the glass but I
didn't succeed. All the people kept looking I got scared and
cryed soon the nurse came and took all the babies back to

their mothers. After that my father came to see me and my mother. He couldn't stay for long but long enough to name me since everyone in my family name begain with an "M" they named me Maurice. Soon my father left then my mother ask me did I like my name. Sence I couldn't talk I just goo gooed. For four days we stayed in the hospital. The fifth day we were free to go on the way out all the people said pray for me and I'll pray for you their were tears all over the ground and sniffin so we went out the door my father was waiting for us we took a cab home. For the first time I saw: cars, trees, trains, the sun, and even people without white suits on.

## WHERE I LIVED

When we got home their were people siting on stoops and no trees. We went up stairs and all my brothers yelled "hello mom" and scared me so I cryed and cryed soon I was asleep so they put me in my crib when I woke up they were talking about me. I had wet my dipare so I cryed my sister Mary heard me and she said curiously "Whats the matter." "Is your dipare wet" as if I could talk she felt my dipare and it was wet. so she called Martin and said "bring me a dipare please." When I saw Larry he was like a giant to me my house was so clean that their wasn't a speck of dirt anywhere. You could look all day with a magnefin glass and still find nothing. When my sister was changing my dipare I felt her hand it was smooth and gentell. I was hungry and cold so my sister gave me my bottle and covered me up the next day we had company they all wanted to tough me and see me. So all I could see was shadows and then I saw clearer and clearer until I could see prefix when I was two years old I got a play pin and my godmothers son baby played in it with me on day we both wanted the same block so he hit me for it then we started to fight soon we cry. So he had to go. When I was small I was stingy and bad and then it came "Wham" right on my backside I was mad at everyone then and was out to kill any one in my way. For the next few days everything was okay than this man came with his dog. He was a friend of my mother. Martin was playing with the dog the dog bart and I screamed with fear and yelled out but the dog was more scared then I was. My mother, father and their friend ran in the back. They thought that I was about to die or something. I was scared and yelled for about an hour. Soon I was in bed sleeping.

## MY SCHOOL LIFE

After years passed by I got older and older and soon old enough to go to school. When my mother sign me up for first grade I was so happy to go but when I saw my teacher I was so scared of her that when my father ask is she a first grade teacher I said "NO." But she said yes the first day was easy but the next three day it was awful I had to rigth read do aritmetic and even spelling. I was so young that I didn't even know how to write. So my teacher showed me how to write. It was easy. I started with "A" and it wined up that I was the second best writer in the class I wasn't the best behaved boy but maybe the worse. I always got hit with the ruler and notes went home. And I got the beaten. All the rest of the year I was an angle.

When I got promoted I went too $2^{-1}$ my teacher was a nice lady until one week went passed we had arithmetic like: $4 \times 39 =$ and $6 \times 25 =$. We knew that she was leaving the school so she made it hard on us. One subject after another first: arithmetic, reading, penmenship, social studies, and some paper work. We had so much homework that it would take a hour are more. On holidays we had a party with enough loliepops for each person could get one the best time we had was when we were out of school. When we got in school the teacher hit me and I hit her back. That when I meet the principal we were boddy boddy. In her was to me I wanted to kill her. In time we got better aquatored. Near the end of the year I got notice that I was being transfore to P.S. ——. When I got my reportcard it wasn't pleasant and when I got home I didn't fell pleasant either.

## MY NEW SCHOOL LIFE

When I got transfore to P.S. —— I had a hard time getting in. First they had to get my recordcard then they got me a place to go that took a week by the second week I was in school my teacher was nice and sometimes a little bit wild. We got along okay but not the principal. He didn't like me and I didn't like him either. We got along. He never said anything to me and I didn't said anything to him. In the third grade nothing happened worth telling. In the forth grade I had the means teacher in the school so I was good at first but adventurely I got bad every time she hit somebody and somebody walk in she would act like she loved him she was luck she every got company she was worse then Miss Myaryer the means teacher in the school.

When I got in to the fith grade I had a man teacher he was the ulgyest teacher in the school you couldn't bend over to pick up a pencil without getting hit he hit boys but not girls. He was so strick that he had to leave at the end of the term. When I got into the sixth grade I had the best teach in the school. He was nice enough to show us how to do harder work then we suppose to do so we have better grades in junior high school when we go we should be thankful for him teaching us.

## FUTURE

The rest of this story is about the future of Maurice the rest of this story may be fiction and may not because it never happened yet. I hope you like it it should be good but may be bad.

## THE WAY I PLAN MY FUTURE

When I become old enough to get a job I plan for it to be a scienceist. I always wanted to be a scienceist so I could do something for our world. I thing there should be more people who try to help our country than their should be to fight against another country because their well be so much blood that we will have a river of blood so I say more people should talk over their problem that to fight them I learned that in the sixth grade. So thats why most people do not like to fight. They fell safer talking over. And I think it's right too.

## MY FIRST JOB

When I went to my first job as a scienceist. I worked for 6 hours a day. And make 150.00 dollars a week. I have to make a living on my money. So when I got home I saw a hunderd dollar bill laying on my dresser with a note saying from a buddy "I'll pay you the rest later.

The book fascinated and amazed me. Maurice was eleven, had never tried to write a story before, asked no help, and handed me such an extraordinary piece of work. I wanted him to continue and develop his theme, elaborate on the future. He wasn't interested. He had said what he felt and wanted to move on to another book, an adventure story. He claimed that his life wasn't over yet and therefore there was no reason to finish the story. I rejected his indifference, not wanting to let such a good thing go. There had to be a follow-up. I ignored my own principle of the author's right to control his work and tried to seduce Maurice into continuing his autobiography. That night I typed up five copies of *The Story of My Life* and gave them to him the next morning. He was impressed, but not as I had hoped. By that afternoon he had sold four of the copies for fifteen cents each and left one on my desk. Sprawled across the final page was "this story shall never be finished."

I had to yield and learn to respect better my own words. As much as I wanted Maurice to revere his work, as disappointing as it was that he kept no copy for himself, it certainly was his right as an author to sell or refuse to complete his own work. It was a false sense of myself as an authority that made me think I had a right to tell him what to feel about it.

Yet Maurice's incomplete autobiography did the class great service. Unanticipated by me four copies were circulated in the room. The other children read Maurice's work, and Michael told me he was proud to own a copy. Slowly other children began to share their work; and decide upon their favorite authors. The children usually didn't show me their work until they had already received several critical opinions from their friends. They did, however, ask me for spelling, or for a new word that they could use instead of an old one they didn't like or found themselves using too often. I gave the children what they asked for without comment.

The children wrote in different styles and genres, and at different rates. Robert Jackson wrote continuously, producing one novel after another. Ralph also wrote continually but with more frenzy, sometimes for hours at a time. He treasured his wild flights of violent imagination mixing television themes and popular music figures with street lore and terror, but refused to have more than four pages of his total output typed or made public. People could read his handscript under his scrutiny but had to yield the book to him, even if they hadn't finished, whenever they went to do something else. Only the first pages of *The Night Club* were typed and distributed as a sort of sampler of his work.

# THE NIGHT CLUB

A long black limazne pulled up to a stop. It stopped to a night club on 93 St. called the Hot Spot. There came out an nice dressing man. He was dressed in a blue suit black hat and shoes. The streets were dark, the streets lights were busted. You could hear young teenagers cursing. Then from the night club you heard rock and roll music. The nice dressing man walked into the Hot Spot and took off his coat and hat. The teenagers began to move around to the Hot Spot. The owner of the Hot Spot was Arther. When Arther seen the teenagers he called the police. The young man was back stage. As the rock and roll was over (the music) the announcer came up and said "Ladies and Gentlemen the moment you have waited for . . . the king off the twist Chubby Checker." The young man was Chubby Checker. The aduance cheered and applauded. Then Chubby Checker san "Let's Limbo Some more." Then the addauance made him sing the twist. When Chubby got through he had to sign autographs. Because all the fans rush up to him to shake his hands. It was 12:00 time for the Hot Spot to close. The annouser told them there was a big line of stars coming up tommrow. As the people came out police arrived to stop the teenagers from robbing the people. The next day the electric people came to fix the lights but as they came the teenagers took out their knives and sticks and chased the people away. Soon they came back with the police. But the police didn't scare them, the gang fought back. But they didn't win, the police won. This made the gang mad so they got another gang called the Dukes. The Dukes and Raiders ran back to 93 St. There they drove the police back. They had gards there to see if they'll come back. It began to get dark. Soon it was 8:00 P.M. Time for the Hot Spot to open. The Raiders walked back to the Hot Spot. The Hot Spot was in a good neighborhood, around a lot of good stores. But the Raiders always broke into some of stores. Soon big limaznes drove up. In the car was Joey Dee, Dee Dee Sharp, Chubby Checker, Bobby Ridel, Little Eva, Elvis Presly, and Murry the K. The Raiders decided to get some dough. When the men got out the car they attacked them. The fight was on. Fist were flying. Movies Stars were fighting like pro-boxers. After awhile the gang retriated. And the stars went inside of the Hot Spot. "It sure is an hot spot" joked Elvis. Soon Murry the K was on stage. His show (the show he was broadcasting on) was an oldie but Goodie show. The small club was packed. Extra chairs were in the club. "Now folks here is the one and only Joey Dee and the starlighters." Joey and and starlighters sang the perpermint twist. Then Murry the K introduced Elvis Presly. He sang his new hit song Girls Girls

Girls. One Raider came in and put a dime in the record machine. Then he played palaside Park. That intoraped the singing. And everyone was annoyed. Elvis was quick to lose his temper. He ran down the stage and ran up to the boy and socked him in the jaw, then he used his getuar and whoped him over the head. After that he kicked him out side. Then he got the show over (his part). Soon the show over and the stars went home.

Alvin wrote only through inspiration, which came too infrequently to prevent constant restlessness and self-doubt. Sam had to copy a war story into one of the binders under his own name before he had courage to write something of his own. Michael and Maurice constantly conferred with each other as did Sonia and Anastasia. There was no end to the variations of mood and tempo with which the children wrote. Some children chose not to write, and there was so much else for them to do that, since I never made a moral issue of it, there was no problem over it.

Robert Jackson put his first novel on my desk one morning and retreated as several other boys gathered about me. They wanted me to read the book immediately and see my reactions. I obliged.

## A BARBARIAN BECOMES
## A GREEK WARRIOR*

One day, in Ancient Germany, a boy was growing up. His name was Pathos. He was named after this Latin word because he had sensitive feelings. In Ancient Germany, the Romans had their vast empire. Everyone in the county was to be a Roman Citizen, speak Latin and learn the Roman customs. Now Pathos, he had a large temper, and he was stubborn. He wanted his people to be free; do as they wish. But his mother had told him, not to stand up against a Roman, or say anything smart, for they will slay him. He grew up fine looking, handsome, but not strong, he was weak and sickly. When he got about 18 years old his mother was killed by a Roman soldier who had hated his family. He was mad at this! So he set out alone on foot. He went to Greece. He was walking down the road lethargectly. Then, from behind, a whip hit him on the back! He fell on his chest, dazed by the

* Copyright © 1967 by Robert George Jackson, III.

slash of the burning whip. He couldn't tell wheater he was
bleeding, dying or what. Then the daze suddenly went away.
Then he could hear the Latin words that he had learned. It
was the Emperor of Rome! But he didn't know it. He got up
an fought like a beast!

"Surrender or die—oof!" Pathos was so mad that he
didn't even reconize the Roman Emperor. The Emperor threw
a spear and wounded Pathos. He was unconscious. When he
awoke, he found himself in the arena of the Coloseum. The
emeperor commanded him: "Since you are so brave, you shall
fight the two ferces lions in all of Rome! If you win, you shall
go free, dare if you lose, you shall be killed, and your soul will
go to Hades, where the King of dead shall rule over you!"
Those words frightened Pathos. Soon, the two lions came
charging out at him He saw one of the Roman Soldiers, then
he swiped a sword from him. The first lion scared him so
much that it made trip backwards, and fall on his back. He
was stunned . . . then could hear the laughing, and jeering
audience. The lion sprang! This would've been the last of
Pathos, but so lucky, had Pathos been, then when he had had
his sword sticking up, the lion hit the sword, then the lion
fell over, and it was dead. The second lion charged, then
Pathos got up threw the sword, and stabbed the lion to death.
The audience cheered, but the emperor . . . you can tell what
the look on his face was . . .

. . . Then the emperor called for his chariot and rode
away to his castl. And in his room . . . "Why has the Goddess
Minerva of Wisdom and Strength done to me? Why did she
give this Barbarian the strength of luck?" Then the wicked
Emperor had an idea, "He is in Greece! I shall send my
Roman Armies to invade Greece! We will make the Greeks
our slaves! And especially Pathos!" So it was then that the
Roman armies invaded Greece! The war was on! Pathos
watching from Mount Parnassus in Greece saw that the Greek
soldiers were being defeated. So he went and put on some
Greek armor, then he went to war! But the armor was so heavy
for him, that he fell to the ground. A Roman Soldier came
charging at him with a spear, the enemy threw the spear, then,
Pathos held out his shield, then the spear bounced off the
shield, then hit the enemy and knocked him out. Pathos managed to get on his feet. But not for long! From behind, another
enemy clashed him on his helmet and dazed him. His head
was swirling, he lost his temper again! He got up and socked
the enemy out cold!

The emperor was so mad at this, that he went to slay
Pathos himself! Pathos saw him coming, he hit the emperor
with his fist! Two other soldiers came. but he knocked them
down one by one! Soon, the Greeks didn't have to fight,
Pathos was knocking them down as they came into him! But
then he got tired, and they took him down. And in a matter
of minutes the Romans conquered the Greeks. Pathos was
sent back to Germany and he was whiped for a punishment
for what he had done. The Romans put him in prison for
5 years. And when he had got out, he was no longer weak or
sickly, he had grown a beard, and was stronger, and more
powerful than ever. Then he decided that he's going to invade
the Roman empire himself, and free all the countries in it.
But where would he get an army of his own? Then he remembered his brother Peri had an army! Then he ran to the practicing grounds where Peri's men were practicing to be warriors.

There, he found his brother, Peri lining up all the Gauls,
"Peri!" he called, "My brother!" They greeted each other
warmly. Then Peri asked Pathos what has happen to him and
their mother. Pathos told Peri about the adventures he had,
and how he was put in Prison. Then he told him that the
Roman soldiers had killed their mother. Peri was angered at
this, then he too seeked revenge on Rome! Then he called to
his men and address to them: "Why do we have to take orders
from just a small city like Rome? We are a large country!
Let us unite and invade these lands! Let us get back our freedom and burn Rome!" Peri meant those words, but there was
one Ruler who meant more than that, that was Attila! He and
his huns were attacking and invading, destroying everything in
his way! The huns came into Germany, burning down the
villages as they went. Peri and men hid in the trees, but Pathos
stood up and said; "I will not run like a dog, I will stand up
and fight!" They came, and Pathos, madder than ever, fought
at the huns!

Pathos fought the Huns as fiece as a lion! When Peri and
his men saw this, they jumped from their hiding places and
fought with Pathos. The Huns were driven away by the Barbarians! Soon, Peri was so excited about this, that he called to
his men; "Let us destroy. Rome!" And they went out to war.
They got all their shields and swords together then Peri asked
Pathos why didn't he want a shield, then Pathos told him he
would want to destroy Rome with his bear hands. Peri urged
him to take the weapons, so Pathos had to yield. The Barbarians Rode north, where they reached England, they con-

quered all of Ireland and the British isles. They rode south
to France, where they burned down the villages, and cities,
Portugal and Spain were too, conquered. They charged down
to Greece, but went through it. Greece was a poor country,
they didn't want to destroy it anymore. Then, Egypt, turkey,
Runania, they conquered them all! Then they went for Rome.
They were stopped by the strong walls which protected the
Romans. Soon, they retreated, year by year they tried to get
through the walls. But then, one night, Pathos sneaked away
to Rome. Peri heard his brother Riding away, so he after him.
Two guards were at the top of the walls of Rome, they saw
him charging, then one of them shot an arrow at him and
Pathos fell off his horse. He got up, took out his spear, then,
threw it at them, and got two for the prize of one! Peri and
his men saw Pathos wounded, but Pathos didn't mind, he
wanted to get in the walls of Rome! He tore off a piece long
pole, then, ran as fast as he could, he stuck the pole in the
ground, then swung high over the walls of Rome! He let Peri
and his men into the gates! Then Rome was awoke from a
high blaze of fire! The Roman soldiers came out and the
Barbarians were fighting the Romans, while Rome was burning to the roots! The Romans were being crushed. Soon
Pathos was caught and put in chains in a dungon. Then they
took him out, and put in a cave, where the alligators were
who ate all kinds of people!

The alligators were trined not to attack the Soldiers, but
the alligators didn't eat for a year and were starving. The
soldiers whipped Pathos, and roughed him up, then Pathos
was still strong enough to move his feet, so he kicked the
enemies into the swampy waters, and the alligators had their
feast. Meanwhile, Peri and his men were slaying and conquering. Then Peri looked for his brother, Pathos, but couldn't
see him anywhere! Soon, the Emperor of Rome sent his most
biggest, strongest, and most powerful army to battle the Barbarians. The Barbarians were being drove out of Rome. Now
Peri didn't know where to look, so in anger, he ran to the
palace of the emperor of Rome. two guards attacked him,
but he took out his sword, and chopped their heads off! He
crashed into the Emperor's chamber, and held his sword next
to the emperor's neck and said; "I will kill you, if you don't
tell me where my brother is!" The emperor had to yield and
told him he was in a cave with the alligators.

Peri raced out of the palace, and went to the cave. He
saw his brother, Pathos, dying. He took off the chains and

started to get out, but ten Roman soldiers surrounded them!
Then, Peri and Pathos were fighting and struggling to get out.
The Roman soldiers were trying to throw the two brothers in
the swampy waters of the alligators, but didn't have a chance.
Instead, most of them went in theirselves.

Outside, Peri's men are fighting hard. Some killed, some
wounded. Rome was burning to the roots. Men, women, and
many children were killed. The barbarians were being driven
out of Rome, but, Rome was up in flames, so they used
torches to conquer the Romans.

The city of Rome burned to its last. The Romans were
finally conquered, after over a hundred years of ruling. Pathos
and Peri conquered the soldiers in the cave too. A few years
later, Pathos went to Greece. He liked the country for its
buildings, sculpture, and art. The Greeks believed in Gods,
such as; Zues, Hera, Iris, Artemis, Apollo, Hermes Posiedon,
Ares, Kronos, Dionysus, Hespheastus, Pan, Pluto, and Athena.
He only believed in one god, because his mother was taught
christianity and secretly taught it to him. On the road to
Greece, Pathos met a blind man. The blind told the barbarian
that when he gets to Greece, he will fight two thieves and
defeat them, then, he will become a soldier and fight in the
Persian war.

Pathos thought it over, so he asked: "Who has told you
this?" The blind man replied, "Hermes, the fathful messenger
of the Gods." Pathos just laughed and continued his journey.
Soon, he came to the city of Marathon in Greece. He was
walking down the dirty streets when he heard a cry for help.
Then he saw two men running from the King's palace and
tried to stop them. They threw knives at him, but missed.

The thieves ran upon a hilltop, hoping they lost Pathos.
But he jumped out of the bushes and attacked them. One of
them swung out at him, but he blocked it with his shield.
While the other caught him from behind. He knocked Pathos
down, then was ready to finish him off. Pathos kicked him
off, then, ran for his sword and shield. The drew their swords
and shields to do battle with Pathos. This was a fight! Pathos
was wounded, and his apponnents weren't. And every time he
swung at one, he would have to watch out for the other.

One of them pierced his shield with a sword. Now Pathos
only had his sword and his chain mail suit. He tried to pierce
their shields too, but his sword broke. Then, he got mad! He
tore off the branch of a tree and knocked them both out. Then
he saw a charriot with a band of Greek Soldiers following.

Then he got his stick ready to defend himself, but the King of
all Marathon told him; "Halt! By what name are you called?"
Pathos wouldn't tell him, because he didn't have a name. The
Romans had called him a Roman word. Then the King got
restless, "Well, speak up! Who are you?" Still not an answer.
"Do you not speak the Greek language?" Then Pathos decided there was nothing else to do but tell them. "I am Pathos
of Germany." Then the King said surprizingly, "Pathos?" All
the soldiers laughed at this. Then Pathos told them the whole
story of his adventures, and how they crushed the Roman
empire. Then the King said, "You are a barbarian, but you
and your men saved all nations from Roman rule. I take you
to my palace, and we will have a feast, and a sacrifice to the
Gods! It is the will of the Gods." Pathos didn't believe in
junk like that, but he had to go through with it. The King
called him μέγας megas, which means large. The King had
called him that, because he was large in strength, and had a
large temper. There, in the palace were many invited people.
There was a big feast, and sacrifice to Zeus, king of the gods.
Other people made sacrifices to other gods like Apollo, god of
archery, music, and poetry, Hermes, god of luck, and the sign
of medicine, and Athena, goddess of wisdom. The King asked
Megas to make a sacrifice to a god. "Make your sacrifice to
the god you like!" But then, Megas said, "There is only one
God, and that is the Lord Christ." "Lord Christ?" Everyone
laughed at Megas. The King ordered Megas be slayed for the
insult of the Gods! But just then, the guards came running in.
"The Persians are attacking again!" After 20 years of planing,
the Persians were finally ready. The King sent out more of
his armies before the Persians burn more of Greece. Megas
was lose, he got some armor on, and then went to fight.

The war was still on! Greek temples were being destroyed, villages, even cities! Marathon was being destroyed
by the Persians. The news came to Athens. Then Athens sent
out their war ships to attack the Persians on sea! Athens
helped Marathon to defeat the Persians, and Pericles the
Athenian leader helped his army defeat the Persians and the
Persian rule, and the Persian empire. After the Persians were
driven out, Athens was rebuilded more glorious than ever
under Pericles. Megas was made a Greek warrior, and those
many adventures were not forgotten.

I put the book down. Robert's tale of Pathos, a barbarian
Christian during the time of Periclean Athens was as impres-

sive as it was inaccurate. Pathos-Megas was alive for me, a weakling grown powerful and blessed with "the strength of luck." Robert's voice, which he hardly ever used in class, was clear and resonant in his writing. Alvin, Maurice, Michael, Reginald, and Leverne crowded about my desk. They had already read the book and formed their judgments, but they wanted to hear what I had to say.

Robert had retreated to his desk and was drawing. His head was only a few inches from the paper, and his shoulders were hunched up.

I didn't know what to say or do. The story moved me, and I was thrilled and flattered to see things we had spoken of in class so beautifully transformed. Yet I didn't want to talk about it; my feelings at that moment overwhelmed and embarrassed me. I muttered something about needing to think about the book and walked away from my desk. The children understood that type of praise and asked for no other response.

Later that day I spoke with Robert and told him that the book was good, so good that I wanted to take it home one night to read with the care and attention it demanded. I asked his permission and he shyly nodded assent. Then he asked me for another binder to begin a new book.

By the time I had reread *A Barbarian Becomes a Greek Warrior*, thought out my criticisms, and reconstructed a plausible historical context for the work, Robert was deep in the Scandinavian night, reshuffling the characters in *The Ring of the Nibelungs*. He told me he was no longer interested in his first book, and I let it go at that. But the class was proud of it, and it passed into our library.

Over the year Robert matured as a writer. His grasp of situation and character deepened, and he became more able to control the plot and structure of his work. It is hard to believe that Robert's final illustrated novel, *Journey Through Time and Space*, was written by a boy still eleven.

# Journey Through Time and Space*

### By Robert George Jackson, III

# I  STARTING A CAREER

It was October, 1935, when a young man had to leave his home because his parents had passed away.

He was only 18 years old and had to look for a job. His name was George Evans and unknown to him he had a twin brother, but his twin brother ran away from home when he was only 6. George had to make some money, but how? He walked down a lonely street and saw a sign on a bakery shop which needed someone to deliver cakes and things to people's houses.

George knew how to drive a truck, and a good pay like $5.00 a day should suit him just fine. He went in the store and got the job. But then 2 weeks later one day, George had to go to Harlem and deliver a birthday cake. The baker sent George there, and then right after George had gone, he put up another sign that said he needed another deliver man. And the baker said, "He'll never come back from that district, because dopatics, hang around there. I lose more deliver men that way." Not suspecting a thing, George stopped at one of the houses and went in the hall with the cake.

He started to go upstairs but he saw two drunkies blocking the way. "Er, excuse me," he said, "but I have to go through." They wouldn't move an inch, until he felt something sharp in back of him. He turned around and saw another drunky in back of him with a knife. Then he took the cake out of the box and threw it in his face and ran to the delivery truck.

He started the motor and tried to speed away as fast as he could, but 5 drunkies were pulling the tail of the truck, holding it back so that George can't pull out. But wickedly, the drunkies let it go and the truck zoomed away! George pulled the brake and the truck stopped so fast that he went flying out of his seat into a junk yard. Then he was in the hospital. He had made up his mind what he was going to be. He wanted to invent things and show himself famous. He wanted to be a scientist.

## II A FAILING INVENTOR

The next morning George was weaker than a baby. He couldn't move a muscle. Then a nurse came in and he yelled, "Hey! I'm paralized! Do something will you?" Then the nurse said, "Alright, I'll have to give you a needle shot." "Do anything, but get me unparalized!" One minute later, George could move himself. "Say nurse, when do I get out of here?" "About a month." "A month?"

A month later, he was out. Then he still counted on being a scientist. He went to a glass factory where they make glass. He sneaked in and tried to take some glass.

But two men jumped him and kicked him out. Hot tempered, George ran back into the factory and fought the two workers. They kept on kicking him out but he kept on coming in. Then finally they asked, "What do you want? We'll give you anything you want if you just go away!" Then George replied, "All I want is some test tubes, flasks, and other scientist's glass equipment." So they gave him what he wanted and he rented a basement as a lab.

He worked hard day and night to find some things man has never done before. He put a lot of chemicals together, and he saw something that he never saw before. He put 2 chemicals together and saw some gases come up. He inhaled the gases and turned invisible.

He exhaled and became visible again. Then he thought to himself, "With this, I can go and take anything I want with my ability to become invisible." So then the next night he inhaled the chemical again and became invisible. He went to the science shop to take some chemicals, but 2 other crooks were running towards him not knowing he was there. They knocked him down and got away. When George woke up he was in a jail cell. "What am I doing in jail?" he asked. "You're in here for trying to steal some chemicals," answered the guard. Then George finally realized that he had failed. Because you see, every time you exhale, you become visible of this chemical, and it wears off in half an hour.

## III  JUST A TRAMP

George had been in jail for so long, that he lost everything he had. He didn't even have a cent. "Well," he thought, "I guess I'll have to get a job." He went by a restaurant and got

a job as a waiter. One day, a drunky came into the restaurant
and ordered some wine. George brought him his wine then
after he got through drinking it out of the bottle, The drunky
said, "How's 'bout yous an' me goin' to a bar t'night?" George
was afraid he would lose his job if he had been caught drinking. So he said, "Get out of this restaurant, or I'll call the
manager!" With that, the drunken man hit George in the jaw
with his fist and knocked him down. George couldn't take

being pushed around any longer, so he got up and knocked
the drunky down. The drunky got up and pulled out a knife.
George grabbed at the knife and tried to make him drop it.
They both fought for the knife knocking chairs and taking the
worst beatings.

The manager was so afraid that he ran to get the police.
Two policemen came in, and the minute George saw them,
he knew he would have to spend another month in jail. So he
jumped out the restaurant door and ran down the street. The
policemen pursued George around the corner where George
hid in a hallway and the police passed him. "Whew," he
panted quietly, "I'm glad they're gone! But now, I guess, I'm

just a tramp. If I leave town, it won't do no good." So he decided to hide in his basement ex-laboratory. He had been in jail for so long he had forgotten where it was. He strolled along the streets day and night. His clothes were getting raggety and people laughed at him. His mother taught him not to beg, even if he didn't have a penny. And George never did beg. And kids made up a song for him:

> We know a bum who walks down the street,
> In rain, or snow, or slush or sleet
> He can't afford to do anything right;
> 'cause if you see him you'll pop like dynamite!

They made lots more of him like this:

> We know a tramp who walks in the damp,
> Like a dirty, stinkin' phoney ol' scamp.
> He can't afford no money at all,
> Or have a great big party or ball,
> 'cause he's just a big fat slob,
> And never has he gotten a job.

The kids sounded on him every day, and he never did get a decent job. But he still had his mind on being a scientist. To invent things and modernize his country.

## IV  THE MAGIC STICK

Wearily George walked on, wondering if he would find the basement that concealed his laboratory. He came to a building which had a sign that read: "Basement for rent, the man who was here made a secret laboratory out of it has passed away."

George exclaimed, "Passed away?" He ran to the basement and saw that all his chemicals had been taken away! In such fury, he yelled for the landlord! "Where's the Landlord?" Then the Superintendant came down to the basement. "What are you doing here? You've been thrown out!" "For what?" George asked. "You're behind your month's rent!" George lost everything, except for one chemical that the Superintendant saved for him. The Super was even nice enough to give George some new clothes. George started his way up the stairs sadly. But then, feeling sorry for George, the Superintendant let George stay for the night until tomorrow morning. With just a single substance that looked faint, all was lost. He took a stick to stir his chemical up and see what would happen to it. George took the stick out and it was glowing like a wand. It was so bright that he threw it out the window, and it came directly back into his hands like a boomerang. He tried to break off the glowing point of the stick by trying to crush it on the table, but instead, the stick went through the table! He was a success! He could walk through solids with the stick, fly with it, and use it as a weapon.

## V  THE INVENTING CAPER

What an invention! George could now prove himself famous. But he was not the only one who could invent a miracle, because on the other side of the neighborhood, some crooks have invented a radar gun to wipe out the whole police force: "We gotta git our boss outa the State Penetentiary. We can easily get through the walls and wipe all the cops in there."

So that night they made plans for getting their leader out

of the pen. George went to try out his new fly powers. He flew up and hovered over the buildings through the beautiful skylight. And just then, by a coincidence, George got tired and landed at the place where the radar men were. He heard them talking about wiping out the police force and about their radar gun.

He wanted to see this radar gun so he took the glowing stick and stepped through the solid wall. Amazing!

His twin brother was Jack the inventor of the gun that might destroy law and order.

He discovered their plans and learned the radar gun's powers and it worked! He flew to the State Penetentiary where the gang's leader was being held prisoner.

He started to walk through the walls when a guard shot at him with a machine gun! He decided to fly to the warden's office. They sounded the sirens and called every guard to shoot to kill! He couldn't get anywhere without a guard blasting at him. Soon, the crooks came in a black sedan and took out their radar gun. "Okay! Set it up for a good blast at the Pen!"

Radar waves were blasting everything in its way! Even policemen! The crooks got their leader out and drove away.

Several police cars pursued them down the road. "Hey! The cops are on our tails! Let's knock 'em in the water!"

George, flying over the crooks with his magic stick overheard what they were going to do. "I'll have to stop them fast! He dived low over the first police car and radiated it with a protective force-shield. The crooks shot the Radar waves at the police car, but didn't even penetrate the car.

A policeman said gratefully, "Hooray! We've been saved by one of the scientific geniuses!" The crooks looked up in amazement! "Hey! That's my copycat twin brother! Let's shoot him down!" The radar waves came up to hit George, and before you could count to three, the radar wave hit George and sent him hazily through space, then in an instant, he was falling down to a place where no one had been. He descended to the ground unconsciously. He woke up and still had his magic stick, but . . . it was no longer glowing! He tried to walk through a rock, but bumped into it. He was lost now. He'd never find his way home. Then he heard a screeching noise. He turned around and saw from behind the mountains that a giant spider, a hairy black widow spider was attacking him.

He picked up a stone and threw it at it! But that wouldn't work. So he ran away into the rocks, but then he was trapped, caught in the spider's web.

And dangling in the web were skeletons and bones of the spider's captives! He was trapped in an unknown place where there were gigantic monsters where every where you turn, there's no end to danger!

## VI GEORGE DISCOVERS INHABITANTS

The large spider was going to eat George up until and band of tribesmen charged at the spider, trying to skin the spider, but each of them were getting clawed up as they got near. George thought of an escape plan to get out of the web. He snatched up some leaves and some cloth and a stick. He tied to the stick the cloth and leaves then he took a match and lit it. He now had a torch. He burned a hole in the web and jumped out. He ran towards a cave and hid there until things cooled off. Well, he had a torch for a weapon, heat, and light. He had his magic stick in his pocket but it was no longer magic. He was walking through the cave, exploring what was in it until a caveman jumped him and tried to choke him. Struggling for life, George tried to get loose. But the more he struggled to get free of the hold, the tighter the grip on his throat. The caveman's wife came in and saw the sight that made her laugh. Mad with pain, George took the caveman and flipped him over his shoulder!

Then the cavewoman cried instead of laughing. She started to run, but George caught her and asked her questions about the things that had been going on and how the animals became giant size. "There is one of the most beautiful

86

lakes in the world," the cavewoman continued, "It has such beauty that if you get into it, you will think you are the most largest person in the world. But the animals who bathe in there kill anyone who dares to go inside." George thought this over. Then he asked, "What year is this?" The cavewoman replied, "It is the year 6,000,000." George was then stunned by the time he had gone through.

So he asked her more questions about the place and she told him. "The animals around here have been trying to conquer the races of men and are trying to succeed in doing it. A man has developed a serum that would enlarge anything, so he domesticated most of the animals to take this serum and put in the lake."

He told them to bathe in the lake and become larger. The animals knew now that if they preserve this, they would destroy the race of man and have the world to themselves as they did millions of years ago." "But why did the man want to destroy his own people?" "Because he thought that the world was never fit for anything nice, or have any peace instead of wars, and killings." George was stunned at what have happening. So he set to gather around all the inhabitants he could find, because he had a plan.

## VII   GEORGE'S CAVEMAN ARMY

George walked around the rocky country looking to find the band of cavemen who saved his life. He looked all around until then two cavemen jumped him and captured him. They took him to their leader, whose name was Notxam. "Why you trespass over land of Notxam?" George was so afraid that he said, "I . . . can't hardly speak with that spear to my throat."

So Notxam took it away from George's throat and let him speak. "Let me lead you instead of Notxam. I will show you how to defeat the giant beasts." With rage Notxam said, "We have contest! We fight to kill! If I win I stay leader, if you win, you stay leader!"

George picked up a hatchet and Notxam had a club. George swung at Notxam with the hatchet and jumped on him. George tried to flip him over, but Notxam hit him on the

head with the club and knocked George into the lake. Notxam
yelled his battlecry and dived in the water right on top of
George. Notxam took his club and banged George with it,
then he started to strangel George with his bare hands. He kept
on strangling for a half hour until George raised up his hand
and surrendered.

Notxam carried George to shore and then took his club
to kill him but then a messenger came and brought news that
a Tyranisaurus was charging in. All the cave people ran as
fast as they could. By this time, George had recovered and
was steaming mad! He saw the Tyranisaurus coming, so he
picked up a club, dodged out of the way and brought the club
down on the Tyranisaurus' head. But it didn't even daze the
charging beast, so he planned to trick the Tyranisaurus into
going to its own doom. He ran to the lake and swam in the
deepest part. Tyranisaurus came after, but then realizing it
can't swim, it drowned. George came out of the lake and
caught Notxam. "Okay, Notxam. Now I am the leader! I have
tricked the Tyranisaurus to drown itself." This time, Notxam
was going to finish George for good, so he took George and
tried to throw him off a cliff, but stumbled and fell off himself. So now George had these bands of uncivilized people.
He could now study and train these people to destroy the giant
beasts and save the race of man.

# VIII  THE SECRET OF
# THE ENLARGING LAKE

George and his men went on an expedition to find the
enlarging lake so that they can analyze it. They came a few
miles then when a giant bee struck one of the men and killed
him. They started throwing spears and shooting arrows at the
giant insect. George took a hatchet and threw it at the bee and
split it right through the head and killed it. Several men were
killed so they had to run the next few miles or they would have
caught the poison. They came to the enlarging lake, and on
the other side saw some giant beasts. George examined the
water of the lake and saw that it had an ingredient in it. He
made a simple microscope and examined it under high power.
Then he looked around and found a serum jar. He sniffed the
insides of the jar and found out that it had the same fragrance
as the water in the lake had. He spotted the skeleton of a man
laying right next to the jar and the fingerprints matched that
on the jar. Then he thought to himself. "That skeleton must
have been the mad scientist who invented this crazy serum.
And the animals must have killed him and kept the serum to
themselves. This skeleton must be at least a hundred years
old." Then George found a watch on the wrist of the skeleton.

"A 20th century watch of my time. This man must have been living in the 1900's." George dipped his powerless stick in the lake and nothing happened. And still George couldn't figure out why his stick didn't work in this dimension.

# IX  THE WAR BETWEEN MAN AND BEAST

George studied all he could about finding out about this primitive race of people. He solved the question of how the animals enlarged, but . . . there were still questions to answer. He thought to himself, "How did the dinosaurs develop to return back to the earth, how did the cavepeople come back, and what happened to the 20th century people, and what happened to their atomic weapons?"

All these questions had to be answered, even why doesn't his magic stick work in this time and place?

George planned to solve all these questions, but fast. He wanted to get back to his own time and place too, but without his magic sticks powers, he was helpless. George and his men went to the lake again. And out of the lake came a giant spider. All of his men retreated, but George was determined to stay and fight this spider. He took a spear and threw it at the giant insect, but didn't hurt it. Then a brontosaurus attacked the spider and fought wildly. The spider killed the brontosaurus and came after George again. George knew that this speciman couldn't be killed, so he ran far into the woods with his men. The spider came fast. One by one it was killing each man. Soon, a giant turtle was in front of them which the spider was in back. They were trapped! George desperately pulled out his magic stick and prayed that it get its powers back. But it didn't work.

But then the spider touched it and it started glowing again! Just as the spider was going to poison him, he held up stick and flew upward.

Out of reach of any monster, George landed at a clear, cool lake and rested. So exhausted, but fell asleep. Soon he was awakened by loud screams that a giant Pteranodon made when it swooped down and snatched up a small cave baby. George got up and got his knife and forgetting about his magic stick, he pursued the gigantic prehistoric bird.

The Pteranodon went across the sea towards an unknown island. George went into the water and swam after the Pteranodon. But suddenly, a giant red crayfish jumped out of the water and clutched onto the Pteranodon's neck and pulled it in the waters with its claw. Struggling to get free, the Pteranodon let go of the baby and let the baby sink into the waters. George swam for the baby and rescued her. Then George was determined to find out the truth where these gigantic and prehistoric beasts came from. So he told his tribesmen that they were going on an expedition to that little isle across the sea, the Monster Isle!

# X  THE EXPEDITION TO THE MONSTER ISLE

You wouldn't think that George was just weak mere, clumsy youth now. His hair had grown long as the other primitive tribesmen. And he had the strength of a bull. He looked exactly like a Cro-Magnon Man. He was determined to find out how those gigantic beasts built their civilization in the large world. George and his men set out in a boat across the sea to the monster island to illuminate all the gigantic inhabits there. Days passed on, as the boat rocked over the restless sea. Suddenly something bumped the boat's hull. And then, out of

the waters came a giant brontosaurus-looking monster with swimfins! It was called an Elasmosaurus! It almost turned the boat over, until George took out his magic stick and tried to disintigrate the monster, but the glowing power was gone! He had his knife with him but he took a poison spear just in case. He jumped overboard into the waters and attacked the beast underwater.

The monster tried to bite him but he blocked the bite with his spear. The monster tried to flee in panic so George pursued the beast to kill him for good.

The Elasmosaurus swam in an underwater cave where it lead to nowhere. George swam up to the surface to get some air and his boat was gone! George had to get to shore fast. The Elasmosaurus attacked George by surprize and caused George to get mad. He took his poison spear and threw it at the Elasmosaurus neck.

The beast floated in the water dead, but that still didn't save George from being endangered. He swam to some rocks and climbed to the top. George looked over the horizons for his lost vessal. He couldn't see how the boat could leave in such a hurry. He lay there and slept the whole night until in the morning he was awakened by that same bird cry. The Pteranodons had attacked him again. His glowing stick didn't work, so he took out his knife and tried to fight back. The Pteranodon tried to grab him, but he killed it. Another attacked him, and this time it was even larger.

The gigantic Pteranodon tried and tried to sweep up George with its claw and take him to its hideout. George fought fiercely among the rocks and tried to keep them away from him. He thought there was no hope left in fighting the fierce beasts but kept on fighting to keep his life. They kept on hovering after him until he got tired of fighting and dived into the water and swam for shore. He walked around the creepy island looking for a safe spot to stay, until he came to a steep cliff. He discovered at the bottom of the cliff were millions of bones of dead men. Plus he saw giant eggs in the holes. Then he thought to himself, "Those must be the eggs of the giant beasts that roam this isle. I'll destroy the eggs now while they're small." So he climbed down the steep cliff and crawled through the bones roughly. He picked up a stone and sharpened it. Then he took a stick and tied it to the stone and made a hatchet. He now had two weapons, the knife and hatchet. He went towards an egg and with all of his might, swung the hatchet and broke the egg in two. Then he destroyed another and another until they were all destroyed. But suddenly, he heard a herd of Triceratops coming his way. "These must be the Triceratops' eggs!"

So he ran as fast as he could to climb the cliff, but it was no use. He could not get back up. The herd of Triceratops came at him, until then he saw from above him that same menace he had met before, it was the giant spider! The hairy beast put down one of its fangs to grab George until then his magic stick started glowing again, just as before. He held his stick up, and lifted from the ground away from the two menaces. When he got about a mile away, the stick lost its power again and he fell to the ground with a bump. When he recovered to his senses he realized what had happened. "Every time I get near that giant spider, my stick glows again. I've got to find the truth about all this." It would soon be night, and in the night the monster Isle is cold and all the beasts come out. George walked through the dark wilderness finding the giant tracks of the black spider.

Soon, he came into a valley, where he saw a giant cobweb and in it lay the bones of dead bodies. He looked around to find the giant menace that had done this.

It was finally night, when George forgot about all the

danger there was. He laid down and went to sleep. No sooner was George sound asleep than he was snatched up off the ground by a tentacle.

He awoke and saw that he was in the clasp of a spider.

The spider started to sting him, but a Tyrannisaurus attacked the spider and chomped off the tentacle that had caught George.

But when one of the spider's arms went off, George fell towards the ground. But the glowing wand reacted to air and lifted George into air flying.

George flew towards the spider, and with his hatchet chopped off its head and killed it.

Now that the spider was dead, the Tyrannisaurus attacked George. He took his wand and blinded the Tyrannisaurus. Now George wanted to find the truth about this spider who had been in connection with the powers of his wand. Suddenly he saw a liquid flow from the spider's neck. He put his wand near it and it stopped glowing. He put the wand away from it and it started glowing again. He knew where to go to find the truth, back to the cavemen to get the truth. He took a large sample of the liquid and flew back to where the home of the future-prehistoric people lived.

# XI THE TRUTH

By the time George got back, it was morning. The huts and caves looked all alike, because these people copied their homes from others. He flew into a cave that was so dark, that he needed his glowing stick for light. He looked all around the cave desperately looking for the people who lived there. There was an open fire and some meat cooking on it, so they had to be here. Suddenly he heard footsteps behind him. He turned around to see that it was the same couple he had met before. The cavewoman smiled in an evil grin. "Kill the one who has the magic power of light, flight, and courage." The caveman obeyed the woman's command and attacked George with a giant club. George waved his wand, but the caveman knocked it out of his hand. George kicked the club out of his hand and jumped him. They wrestled all over the floor until the cavewoman picked up the club and tried to hit George with it but failed and knocked out her own husband. George got up and snatched up the club away from the woman and demanded the truth about the whole origin of this futuristic place and the giant and prehistoric animals. The woman confessed, "I may as well confess the truth to you. Long ago in the 30th century, a scientist explored various parts of the world. He traveled to the arctic pole in his space ship and landed in a cave. He put on a weather-proof suit and discovered that in the cave, frozen stiff in suspended animation were a man and a woman, prehistoric people were in there over a million years! He took out his anti-freeze gun and defrosted the prehistoric couple, and instantly they came to life! They started to attack him but he switched to his freeze gun and stopped them stiff. He took them back to his lab secretly and experimented on them. He had many other experimental things he had found, like insects, the bones of prehistoric beasts, birds, amphibians, reptiles, and species. Later he invented an unknown chemical.

Unknown to him this was the enlarging chemical that was poured into the lake. One day he started to examine the serum to discover its powers. He went outside and took a bee with him. He dipped some of the serum on the bee, and in an instant, it grew into the size of a buffalo and attacked the scientist and killed him. The serum spilled into the lake and dissolved. All of the scientist's species escaped into the lake and enlarged themselves. The two prehistoric people were exposed to the anti-freeze ray and retreated back to the arctic cave and froze stiff in suspended animation once again. A few thousand years later, the earth changed. So did the sun. It was now red. All the peoples on the earth were dead.

Their weapons and machines destroyed by the enlarged creatures. The giant beasts took over the earth and stalked it for years until out of the caves and holes in the earth, prehistoric creatures came back to life as if by magic. Now there looked as if there was no hope at all. But then, a giant spider was exposed to the anti-freeze ray and had been more powerful than any of the monsters on the earth. It went to the Arctic and melted all the ice and snow there. It revived the two prehistoric man and woman from suspended animation.

The couple fled for their lives from the giant insect down to the south. There their generations started to spread. Now we are descendants of those very prehistoric couple." Amazed at the history of this, George decided, "There's not a thing I can do now. I guess there's no hope of earth becoming a better world now. Either it's up to the people of this race, or up to God." So, wearily George left the cave.

# XII  THE RETURN OF GEORGE'S CAVEMAN ARMY

In the morning George was going back through his own time. But he wanted to take his last looks at the war-torn earth

and pity it. He went into the deep woods and stopped for a
rest. Suddenly he heard loud footsteps all around him. He
stood up and saw his band of cavemen he once had. Suddenly
one of them spoke. "Some leader, great you are, you abandoned us on the boat when we were attacked by sea-dinosaur.
We are now going to kill you, because you are not our great
leader like Notxam was." They all jumped on George and
knocked him down. He got red-hot mad and yelled, "If I'm
not the great leader, you will laugh, but I will show you that I
am the great leader, because I challenge you all to a duel!"
With that, he took off his shirt and jacket and stood defiant
furiously before the men. They all jumped him at the same
time, but got knocked off at the same time. He punched,
kicked, and flipped all the men until they all gave up and
agreed that he was their greatest leader, the leader of the magic
wand. George thought, "Now that I have my army back, the
least I could do before I leave in the morning, is try to
decontaminate that lake to get all the serum out of the water
to stop the regrowth of animals.

So they set out an expedition to disintegrate the hidden
formula in the lake.

# XIII  CRO-MAGNONS VS.
PITHECANTHROPUS MEN

They kept on their bold journey through miles and miles
of attack and ambush caused by the giant animals. They came
to a large field where there was a large hole. George examined
it and saw that it was the house of a field mouse. Then they

heard a screeching noise, somewhat like that of a mouse. They turned around and saw a field mouse as large as a dog! It attacked several men and killed them.

The men fought hard at this giant rodent with hatchets, spears, and arrows. Soon all the men ran and hid. All except for George.

He tried to run, but realized the king-sized mouse was too fast for him. He tripped over a rock and fell. Stunned by surprize, he thought he was a gonner for sure until a giant hawk attacked the mouse and fought it.

Meanwhile, coming to his senses, George and his tribesmen sneaked away to the swamps. Now all George had was 20 men. In the first place, he had 30. They walked through the marsh of the swamps day and night without food or water. Finally, George could no longer endure this. And refused to go on. His men refused to let him go and argued all in the swamps. George was so mad that he forgot he was standing on a snake, a giant snake. The snake jumped up and George flipped to the ground unconsciously. The giant snake killed 10 more men and frightened the rest away. It spotted George recovering and went to kill him.

He threw a spear at the monster, but it didn't work. He hurtled a hatched at it and still no use. Since that didn't work, there was only one thing to do. His magic wand had come in handy. "This is my chance to see if my wand has any electro-shock power in it," he thought. So he waved his glowing stick and in an instant an electro power beamed out and struck the giant snake dead. After the snake was dead, George and his men made poison knives out of the snake's fangs. They also stripped off some of the skin and used it for protective shields against any other attackers. They continued their mission. After several hardships, they came to the enlarging lake and found an enemy tribe guarding it. George and his last 10 men charged at them and attacked!

Through all the battles, all of George's men were wiped out completely. George saw that he was going to be killed by the fierce Pithecanothropus men. George waved his magic wand and flew up into the skies, hovering over the enlarging lake, and said to himself, "Now I shall illuminate the center of giant life!" and with that, he shot a disintegrating ray in the lake and evaporated all the water there. And right after he did that, he disintegrated into the skies. Let's go back thousands of years through time and space when in 1935, the gang of crooks who broke their leader out of the penetentiary and were pursued by the police when George flew after them and was hit by the radar beam. The crooks shot the radar beam and blasted all the police cars over the bridge. In an instant, a flying figure appeared in the sky. It was George! He shot a beam of light at the cars and saved them all from falling into the water. After that, he disintegrated the radar-gun, and melted the tires on the bandit's car and captured them.

## XIV  FINALLY ON HIS FEET

The next day, in the warden's office, George received a double-reward for his methods in science, capturing the crooks, and rescuing several police. The warden greeted him and thanked him for all he had done for his country and his world. "George Evans, because of your scientific ingenuity, you have made our country more famous than ever. We will not use your invention right away, because the earth is not ready for such a precious gift, but we will preserve it. But maybe in the future, we will try to stop this scientist and giant beasts from ruling our world.

**THE END**

ABOUT A MONTH after the trip to Cambridge I found a notice in my school mailbox. It stated that if by Thursday (it was then Monday) the children in my class could get signed parental permission slips we could take a trip to the Metropolitan Museum of Art, receive a guided tour of the special children's exhibit on archeology, and get free subway fare. Reluctantly I told the children, who were delighted with the chance to spend a day out of school.

I wasn't so enthusiastic and didn't feel that "we" were ready to take a trip, that is, I was afraid to travel with my thirty-six children and imagined the most chaotic and embarrassing scenes. But the children wanted to go and so we went. Twenty signed permission slips were returned by Wednesday. On Thursday morning Maurice handed me the other sixteen slips bearing signatures that resembled each other's and his. I let it pass and we set out.

The first problem I had to face was how to walk through the streets with the children. Should the class stay in line, double file, holding hands as I had done in school fifteen years before on a similar trip to the Metropolitan Museum? I could insist and spend the day trying to keep the children in line, but to what point other than impressing the people we passed with my authority and the children's obedience. I wanted the children to observe the city and enjoy the trip, so let them walk naturally with whomever they pleased. We moved as a casual group, and though we may have upset some people the walk from the school to the subway was leisurely and pleasant. The train ride from 125th Street to 86th Street was very quiet. The children huddled together, avoiding the white riders coming from the Bronx to spend a day downtown.

We emerged from the subway at 86th Street and Lexington Avenue and walked toward the museum. At Park Avenue Marie came up to me and said:

"Mr. Kohl, where are we? In Long Island?"

"Marie, this is Park Avenue and Eighty-sixth Street."

She looked at me as if I were mad, then went to Pamela and told her Mr. Kohl said it was Park Avenue. The rumor spread through the class until finally a delegation of boys headed by Sam and Ralph approached and challenged me to

101

prove it was Park Avenue. I pointed to the street signs and
they looked as if they wanted to cry.

"But where is Harlem? I live on Park Avenue—where are
the tracks?"

I pointed north. The children looked but could only see
Christmas trees stretching up to 96th Street. Harlem wasn't
visible. They looked up at the sign again and we made our
way to Madison Avenue.

"But, Mr. Kohl, our bean school is on Madison Avenue."

And then to Fifth and the museum where we were greeted
by a tall young woman wearing a name tag proclaiming that
she represented the Junior League. The exhibit was fascinating—things to turn, push, and pull, pictures of Sumer
which we were studying in class, Egyptian remains, undersea
diving equipment, salvaged gold and weapons. The kids forgot
about Park Avenue and were ready to rush in. But first we had
to pause and learn about artifacts, layers, some other things I
couldn't grasp—the guide's vocabulary was as stunning as her
legs. She sat down on a stool and spoke to the children who
crouched uncomfortably on the floor. Marie whispered to me.

"Mr. Kohl, tell her to pull her skirt down. It isn't decent."

The kids were bored after fifteen minutes. Ralph and
Robert Jackson wandered off to explore for themselves. Alvin
and Michael started pushing each other. Brenda started a fight
with Carol. After half an hour I was the only one who even
pretended to listen. Twelve o'clock rescued us. It was time for
lunch, but rather than risk the chaotic conditions in the museum lunchroom I took the class out to lunch in the park.
It was cold but private. The children spread out, ate, and
talked.

I hadn't brought any lunch, and they insisted that I share
theirs. After they were finished the boys decided to race. They
asked me to mark out a course and for the rest of the afternoon the children raced, roamed over the park, talked. Exhausted, we returned to school at four o'clock.

I couldn't forget the children's response to Park Avenue
and 86th Street and because of it instituted my Friday trips.
A week after we had gone to the museum I made a general
invitation to the class to take a drive with me down Park
Avenue. Seven children took me up and at 3:15 on Friday
we set out from 120th Street and Park Avenue, passing the
covered markets at 116th, the smelly streets down to 110th,
and the dismal row upon row of slum clearance projects all
the way to 99th Street. On the left of us loomed the elevated
tracks of the New York Central Railroad. We ascended from
99th to 96th, reaching the summit of that glorious hill where

the tracks sink into the bowels of the city and Park Avenue is metamorphized into a rich man's fairyland. Down the middle of the street is an island filled with Christmas trees in winter and flowers during the summer, courtesy of *The* Park Avenue Association. On either side of the broad street opulent apartment buildings, doormen, clean sidewalks. The children couldn't, wouldn't believe it.

"Mr. Kohl, where are the ash cans?"

"This can't be Park Avenue."

"Mr. Kohl, something's wrong . . ."

It was Pamela, not angry but sad and confused. We passed the gleaming office buildings further downtown. I was about to comment but sensed that the children were tired and restless. They had had enough and I had too. We returned to Harlem and then I drove home back downtown. The city was transformed for me through the eyes of the children. I saw a cruel contradictory New York and wanted to offer something less harsh to the children. Perhaps my apartment between Park and Madison Avenues, just a mile from the school yet in the white city, could offer something less strange and hostile. I wasn't sure. The principal and other teachers had warned us about getting too friendly with the children, of transcending the traditional formal distance between pupil and teacher. They told me it wasn't "professional" to develop relationships with the children outside the context of the school. Besides, one of the older teachers had warned me, "You never can tell what 'these' children might do" (or, as I almost added, what the neighbors would say). No, I couldn't tell, but the children couldn't tell about me either. That was our greatest problem: we didn't know each other's lives.

Warily, yet convinced that it was right, I invited the class to visit my house the next Friday—it must have been toward the middle of December, Alvin, Maurice, Leverne, Robert Jackson, Pamela, Grace, Brenda W., and Carol accepted. It was quite a squeeze but we all made it into the car and to my apartment which was on the fifth floor of a walk-up. The hall door was locked, the mailboxes as well as the buzzers worked. The children noted these wonders, then made the five flights with ease. I had one large room crammed with books, records, pictures, statues—things I had picked up at college and in Europe. There was a record player, tape recorder, radio. The place was in chaos, but I knew where most things were.

The first thing that struck the children was that it was mine. No parents, sisters, brothers, cousins. They saw how completely mine it was and loved the idea.

I was anxious about what would happen that afternoon—
what the children would do, what we could talk about. Intuitively I knew we all felt the same way, nervous and awkward
but of goodwill. Something would, had to occur to relieve the
tension. It did very quickly. Alvin saw the tape recorder and
asked me if he could work it. I showed him how and the children crowded around. Alvin put the machine on. The reels
spun. Nobody wanted to talk; there was an awkward silence.
I uttered a few inanities, feeling embarrassed, wondering
whether the whole thing wasn't a grave mistake. Maurice,
who was looking through my books, came to the rescue.

"Alvin, sing 'Vic Tanny.' "

"What's Vic Tanny?"

Pamela turned to Alvin who blushed, begged encouragement, and receiving it, sang *Vic Tanny's Gonna Put You
Down*, a song he had made up the year before.

> *Vic Tanny's gonna put you down,*
> *Dum! Dum!*
> *Vic Tanny's gonna put your bones down!*
> *Vic Tanny's gonna put you down,*
> *'Cause they ain't got time to be jiving around.*

Skinny Minny is my sister's name
And I'll always call her the same.
Vic Tanny's gonna put her down,
'Cause her bones are weak and they're turning around.
Dum! Dum!

> *Vic Tanny! . . .*

My brother has a lot of muscle,
He always like to run, jump, and hustle.
Vic Tanny's gonna put him down,
'Cause he ain't worth a penny on that dirty ground.
Dum! Dum!

> *Vic Tanny! . . .*

Mrs. Wrenn she tried to swim,
She tried to play-a-like-a Jungle Jim.
Vic Tanny's gonna put you down,
'Cause her funeral was in the next town.
Dum! Dum!

> *Vic Tanny! . . .*

His mother sent him to the store
And then she conked out on the floor.

Vic Tanny's gonna put her down,
'Cause the smelling salts had to bring her around.
Dum! Dum!

*Vic Tanny!* . . .

Sikie Mikie he tried to run,
He tried to act-a-like-a Peter Gunn.
Vic Tanny's gonna put her down,
'Cause her sikes are dirty and her head is round.
Dum! Dum!

I called Judy and she came upstairs. The girls ran up to
her, drawing her into the circle that had formed around the
tape recorder. The children talked and listened to each other.
They seemed themselves in a way they couldn't in the classroom. I looked and listened, discovering how much I missed
by being up in front of the room, a teacher of thirty-six souls
I couldn't know individually.

Pamela took over from Alvin. Thin, beautiful Pamela, so
much herself, nondefiant and noncompliant, the smallest girl
in the class but the one no other child dared to anger.

PAMELA. Hello, my name is Pamela Reed. I'm at Mr. Kohl's
house and I'm talkin' on a tape recorder and Brenda is
laffin' at me and Carol's wipin' her hands and Margie's
playin' cards and Carol wants to sing and Mr. Kohl's
smokin' a cigarette and Alvin is buildin' bricks and
Leverne is, I mean Maurice is doing nothin', playin' with
Tootsie Roll paper (*giggle*) and Margie say, "Are you
all ready?" (*A record comes on.*)

PAMELA. "Do You Love Me's" gonna sing for us. (*Record in
background.*) You hear it? It's singin' very nice. (MARGIE
*sings along with the record.*) Well now, you heard "Do
You Love Me" sing, so now you wanna hear me sing?

MARGIE. Now, everyone, we will hear "Everybody Loves a
Lover" by—(*pause*) Pamela can't sing so I'll sing for her.

PAMELA. Well listen, how dare you insult me now?
(*Record starts.* MARGIE *sings along with it.*)

MARGIE. Now wasn't that bee-u-ti-ful? I'll punch you in the
face, Pamela.

PAMELA. Let me tell you now, you know Margie she don't
know no better, that's why she always says that, but you
know she's so big I have to let her beat me or everybody
would say, "You let that little girl beat you?" So that's
why I always let her beat me. Next time she start messing
with me I'm going to have to hurt her.
(*Record: "Twist and Shout."*)

PAMELA. Now you just heard "Shake It Up, Baby." You gonna
hear it again, but I'm sorry, oh there was a mistake, it's
"Do You Love Me" (*pause*). Um, you know, it's a state
of confusion at this moment so we don't know yet. "Do
You Love Me" is coming on for real now, so you have
to wait until it comes on. Ready? (*Singing and giggling.*)
Now here's the Wiggle-wobble. Having a good time . . .
the boys are wobbling, the girls are wobbling . . . Grace
doin' the walk . . . Brenda's shakin' it up . . . have to
leave my duties, so, you know how it is. (*There is a
long absence while the music plays in the background.*)
Here comes that horn . . . it's goin' off . . . oh, oh . . .
tsk . . . (PAMELA *clucks while an argument goes on in
the background over* PAMELA *hogging the recorder.
Record* "Everybody" *begins and* PAMELA *sings along,
stops.*) I smell something. (*She doesn't know many of
the words to the song, pretends.*) Margie, wanna talk?
(*There is increasing confusion in the background, something about taking something out.*)

MR. KOHL. Put that down, Maurice! Margie, Margie, we're
all going home in parts if you take it out!
(*"Twist and Shout" comes on accompanied by* PAMELA's
*singing.*)

*From Background.* Mr. Kohl, why don't you wobble?

MR. KOHL. Later, later.

PAMELA. Well since "Shake It Up, Baby" went off, one of
the stars is here. The other star had to stay home, so,
we stars of One hundred and nineteenth we know almost
everything, but it's a pity that some children can't keep
up with us but, you know, some people have it and some
don't.

The afternoon flew. As the children felt comfortable they
began to explore the apartment, look at the pictures, ask about
the books. We talked to each other in a way that I couldn't
yet do in class. The children probed for my interest and my
commitments. They wanted to know what I cared about as
much as I wanted to know about them. I talked about my
writing, about the years I spent in Paris looking for myself,
the joy of discovering that I was a good teacher. The children
wanted to know how I got to Harlem, whether my parents
were still alive, if I had brothers and sisters. I answered, thinking that the children really cared who I was and that it had
never occurred to me that they would. The other teachers
would have repeated that exposing myself to the children that

way was "unprofessional." Perhaps they really would have felt exposed and found their authority threatened had their students known them as human beings and not as "professionals."

Until I found myself talking to my pupils about myself and my life in the context of my home I unconsciously held off from the children too. I avoided answering questions about my private life, even though I felt rejected because the children wouldn't let me into theirs. Talking with the children, taking them home on occasion, seeing them relaxed and playful, I realized how narrow the view from the teacher's desk is. I also realized that any successful classroom has to be based upon a dialogue between students and teachers, both teaching and being taught, and both able to acknowledge that fact.

Taking the children home wasn't always pleasant. One wintry Friday afternoon six children climbed up to my apartment. They were cold and angry. It had been a particularly chaotic day in school, and I had lost my patience. I wanted to be alone and dreaded the thought of taking children home with me. Still, I had given my word that on Fridays the children could come if they wanted to and had to keep it.

I opened the door and growled.

"Throw your coats down wherever you want."

Leverne responded by flipping his coat across the room. It landed on a cabinet, sweeping everything in its way onto the floor. One of my most precious possessions, a fragile pre-Columbian statue, was shattered beyond repair. Tears came to my eyes, then harsh anger. Leverne looked at me and fell to pieces.

"I didn't mean it, see I can put it together. Here's the head."

"Mr. Kohl, he didn't mean it."

Alvin held onto my arm as if to prevent me from hitting Leverne. I looked at them and the other four children whose bearing seemed to be telling me, "See, we knew it would never work out." Then a smile came over my face.

"It isn't worth anything. I'll pick up the pieces while Alvin gets the tape recorder."

Another time, Alvin, Maurice, and Michael walked from the school down to my apartment on a Wednesday afternoon. Their coming was a delightful surprise, and I let them in. They came after school the next day as well, and I'm sure that they could have eaten up the whole week with their visits. I had to explain to them that I needed time to myself and could only see people from the class after school on Fridays. They were angry and told me they would never come to my house again. That Friday the three of them didn't come, though they did the week after. I had to set limits on what I could do as an individual and have always had to balance what part of my life I could offer the children and what part had to remain private.

AS THE YEAR DEVELOPED the class did a lot of writing. I discovered that if the children were allowed to write without being marked, and if they were challenged and tempted by the subject, they wrote with great pleasure. At first it was just a question of writing sentences using the vocabulary and spelling words. The children tested me to see how far they could go, but they really never went very far.

*ineffable:* God is ineffable but Charles is not.

*navigate:* Maurice is so blind his roaches has to do his navigating for him at the rate of a penny an hour (cheapskate).

*symbol:* A rock is a symbol for food to Leverne.

*patricide:* He is the only one strong enough to do patricide in his family.

*fable:* Grace tells good fables becaus she don't like to say anything direct.

*malediction:* I put a malediction on people who steal and run away from trouble.

Some of the children even tried to put many of the vocabulary words together into stories, but they usually were not pleased with the results. The experiment was too artificial.

*Brenda T.*

Once upon a time there was a women and she was real Neat and she was real hip. She could do the two-step, the twist, the mash potato and lot's of other dances. She could talk like beaknick's talk and she had a very nice figer and was good looking.

So one day her niece Nina came to visit her. So her niece brought a chew-wa-wa with her. As soon as Joyce the lady saw the dog she screamed "Get that *animal* out of here!"

So as soon as she sold the dog, she got some goldfish.

Joyce was going to get a glass of water and she saw the

fish in the sink she said, "Where did you get those *animal-cules?*" Get them out right now.

The next day Nina had to write a *essay* on the *biography* of Robert Fulton. She got poor on the subject and the teacher put her in the *sculpture* room and she said, "See if you could be a *sculptor.*

She failed in that to so the teacher said, "You shall take *architecture* and see what you do in this subject." She finally passed a test and she went back home and her aunt Joyce said she would never have her come again.

P.S. This is a bad story.

Then there was the challenge of myth. Every myth or tale has an undiscovered number of possible variants. One day, one of the last during the time we still had readers, the class read a bland retelling of the myth of Demeter and Persephone that underplayed the sexual and violent elements. The theme of the conflicts among mother, daughter, and the man who steals the daughter away from her mother nevertheless penetrated. Whereas the text attempted to present the children with a quaint and prescientific explanation of the seasons, the children saw beyond this to the archetypal human struggles embodied in the tale. They weren't satisfied with the book's treatment of the characters and asked me how Persephone felt about Hades, whether she liked the underworld or was glad to escape her mother. I threw the questions back to the class, asked them how they felt Persephone reacted to Hades, and what sort of a mother they thought Demeter was. There was no general agreement; one girl felt it must have been exciting to live in the underworld, another that Persephone must have been lonely and missed her mother. There were almost as many opinions as children. Thomas C. raised his hand after listening to too many different Persephones being carried away by too many different Plutos.

"Mr. Kohl, which one is right?"

He was truly puzzled. The class quieted down; they wanted a judgment from me. I could sense a contest, the vying for honors based on individual re-creations of collective myths that were Greek tragedy.

"I can't answer directly. Which is right, a happy Persephone or an unhappy Persephone—? is there any right answer to what one must feel? Feelings are more complicated than right and wrong, but let me tell you about how the Greeks treated their myths. They had a holiday dedicated to Dionysus, one of their gods, and for that day one mythical theme was selected, some story of the lives of men and gods. All the people who were interested wrote plays using that same story, as we were really just doing with Demeter and Persephone. There was no one right way to look at the myth, and the winner of the contest wasn't the person who said the right thing. It was the one who expressed his view of the myth in the most beautiful and moving way."

Brenda raised her hand.

"Could we try and have a contest?"

The class wrote (October 11–14):

*Neomia*

One day while Persephone was picking flowers she heard the huffs of horses coming toward her. The other people who were picking flowers ran but Persephone just stood there. There was a man with a long black beard, he was the one who was driving the chariot. He came closer and closer to Persephone until it looked like the wheels were going to kill her. When he picked up Persephone and took her to his kingdom he made her queen. Her mother became so furious that she went to the kingdom where her daughter was and killed the king, the guards, the maids, and the butlers. Her daughter was so happy to see her that she left the kingdom and went back home with her mother. Her mother and her lived happily ever after.

*Brenda W.*

One day Persephone was going to the store for her mother. Persephone was quiet and had a lot of animal friends. While she was walking she saw a chariot. Now Persephone not knowing it was Pluto from Hades the city of death ordered him to stop. After he had stoped he said "my name is Pluto, I come from Hades the city of death." "I am looking for Princess Persephone." Persephone looked startled. "I am Persephone." "Good then come with me." Instead of Persephone going to the store she went with Pluto. Persephone was only 12 years old and Pluto was 85. Imagine Persephone marrying Pluto. He was old enough to be her great grandfather. Demeter, Persephone's mother was getting worried and wondered what took her daughter so long to go to the store. She went out to look for her daughter. She called and called but her daughter did not answer. She gave up hope. She thought that she would never see her daughter again. One day her daughter came home more beautiful than ever. She did not tell her mother what happened. Now Persephone lives happily with her mother.

*Charisse*

I think the story was very good. Here is my idea of the story. One day all the goddesses were setting down play with the flowers. When a man came riding by. He was riding all in red he was the underword god. He stop at the spots where the goddesses were play he grab up Persephone. Persephone said to him at last you have come for me. They had planned this elopment. Persephone mother was mad at this sudden outrage she try to get at the underworld god. but she couldn't so Demeter die because she couldn't see her daughter.

*Margie*

The story would have been more interesting if Persephone could come and stay with her mother for a whole year and then we would have nice weather all year round.

If Persephone had run with all the other maidens she wouldn't have gone down there in the first place and caused her mother so much trouble. If she hadn't eaten those seeds she would have been able to stay up on the Earth with her mother and we would have nice weather all year round, and her mother would be very happy and if the nymph had not been turned to water, she could have told Demeter that Pluto had taken Persephone away.

*Thomas C.*

I think this story would be better if the girl liked pluto and wanted to live with him. But her parents didn't know that and after 4 years destroyed pluto and the girl was sad until she met a beggar and married him. She had ten children but her husband died and she lived happily not married ever after.

*Sonia*

I wish that Pluto didn't want to give up Persephone's and Demeter keep on looking and one of Pluto men kill Demeter. The world had an earthquake and Persephone run away before the earthquake she ran into a New world lots of furits and food a lot of water plenty animals a lot of grass and plenty of people and houses a lot of chtles and she ran off with a man name Johnthan and He married her in the most bueitiful dress they had the most bueitiful house and 10 bueitiful children a maid a carriage and they live happily ever after and Pluto was dead and every body came to her wedding. Everybody wanted one of the kids for a godchild Persephone had five girls and 5 boy one of the girls she named Demeter so she can remember her dear mother who died looking for her and the girls grew up to be some bueitiful princess and the boys the prince the day came when all of them died 97 before they died they toll the story of there wonderful life and Persephone darling mother Demeter

I read the papers to the class and we talked about the variations on the myth. The children were surprised that their interpretations differed so much. As the discussion developed I realized that the children were doing close textual analyses of each other's work, attending to style and content, judging language. They contrasted Brenda's old benign Hades with Neomia's unambiguously evil one, commented on Sonia's baroque style and Margie's peevish contrariness. The discussion flowed freely in no particular direction, the children explored whatever aspects of their writing interested them. I didn't interrupt to restate a point or intrude something that had been missed. That would only detract attention from the myth and destroy the enthusiasm that was building through the children's participation. Such free-flowing discussions, unplanned and unplannable, are essential if the teacher is to discover how to develop material that interests children. Somehow they have a way of assuming form and taking direction. For me what usually happened was that some comment brought things together and at that point I found myself responding naturally and seeing what I as a teacher could contribute. This time it was Kathy who asked.

"Mr. Kohl, can't you think of myths as stories about mothers and daughters, like examples of what happens if you don't listen or do something wrong in the family?"

"I agree, but they're more, they're about man and god, man and his rulers and loves, about conflicts that all people face in their families and religions and countries."

Robert Jackson raised his hand, and I had to stop and honor so infrequent an occurrence.

"Someone told me Christ was a myth. Can't different people have different myths?"

"They can and do, and even at times they use other forms of writing or stories to teach people about life, or just to express the way they look at things."

Charisse became angry.

"But Christ is true. Those Greek things aren't true!"

"Charisse, I don't know what's true so I have to content myself with learning what I can from the way different people express what the world means to them. The Greek myths tell

me something about what the Greeks thought was important
and unimportant, the Bible tells me about the early Christians
and Jews though not much about people today."

The class fell silent, but not with hostility. The children
became pensive. I too remained silent, thought about the words
that had come from my mouth, and waited for something to
happen, for someone to answer. No one did; one boy noise-
lessly set up the chess board, another joined him and made a
first tentative move while two checker games began, books
appeared from desks. Ten minutes passed, no voice was raised
above a whisper. I found myself hoarsely declaring:

"I think it's time for arithmetic."

The next day I read Thurber and Aesop to the class
while introducing the two new words *fable* and *moral*. No
explanation beyond the reading of the fables was necessary.
We compared ancient and modern fables, and discussed the
use of animals and objects, as well as people, to tell a story
and make a point. I then read some Anansi fables and we
discussed irony and *double-entendre*. The children tried to
make up alternate morals for some of Thurber's fables, and
we talked of how the moral can change the whole sense of
a tale.

Then I asked the class to write—they tried and weren't
happy with the results. So then we went back to some of the
Thurber they had liked and did a little analysis. Then they
wrote other fables, some of which pleased them more. In fable
writing two children—Barbara and Thomas C.—found their
métier, and others began to write for the first time.

### Barbara

Once upon a time there was a pig and a cat. The cat kept
saying you old dirty pig who want to eat you. And the pig
replied when I die I'll be made use of, but when you die you'll
just rot. The cat always thought he was better than the pig.
When the pig died he was used as food for the people to eat.
When the cat died he was buried in old dirt.

Moral: Live dirty die clean.

### Thomas C.

Once a boy was standing on a huge metal flattening machine. The flattener was coming down slowly. Now this boy
was a boy who loved insects and bugs. The boy could have
stopped the machine from coming down but there were two
ladie bugs on the button and in order to push the button he
would kill the two ladie bugs. The flattener was about a half

inch over his head now he made a decision he would have to
kill the ladie bugs he quickly pressed the button. The machine
stoped he was'saved and the ladie bugs were dead.

Moral: smash or be smashed

*Barbara*

Once upon a time a girl was walking up the street with
her little brother. Her little brother loved to suck a <u>pacifier</u> all
of the time. One day he met a little girl that loved to <u>suck</u> her
finger. The little boy asked her how does you finger taste? The
lettle girl said it tastes delicious. The girl asked how did the
<u>pacifier</u> taste and the boy said delicious. They traded and the
boy liked the tumb the best and the girl liked the pacifier best.

Moral: Enjoy them all.

*Charles*   THE WAR WITH THE MOON AND
            EARTH

One day the United States sent up a rocket to the moon.
It took the capsule 7 hours to go from the earth to the moon
And when he got there all the moon people saw him and they
sent him back to earth with a note saying we dicarl war on
earth: Moral never sent a rocket to the moon.

*Charles*            THE CAVE MAN MYSTERY

One year about 5 or 6 thousand years ago this caveman
had a lot of funiture then his cave was always being robbed.
And soon he had nothing to wear or no funtire: Moral Never
have to much furniture.

*Desiree*   Feb. 26

Said the devil to the angle I can get more people than
you. Said the angle to the devil "I will bet you two to two.
Then one day a handsome man came walking up the road the
devil and the angle had there eyes set on that man. The bet
was that it be the devil Put a glass of fire at the end of the
road and the angle set a glass of water at the other end. So it
happen to be, the man was thirsty And he went for the glass
of water. The devil was so mad at the lost of his bet that he
through him self in a net for shammery.

The morle is You can catch more people when there hot,
with water. than can Fire

This story is Fony. My Morle
My mind wasn't focasing.

*Franklin*   Feb. 26

Once upon a time there was two men who were always fighting so one day a wise man came along and said fighting will never get you anywhere they didn't pay him no attention and they got in quarrels over and over again. So one day they went to church and the preacher said you should not fight and they got mad and knock the preacher out

Can't find no ending.

The children read their fables to each other, made copies of their work, which they exchanged or pasted on the classroom walls. There were favorite fables, Barbara's two and the one of Thomas C. that had "smash or be smashed" as a moral. But the piece that fascinated the children the most was Franklin's. They wanted to know if his non-ending was an ending. Michael held that "can't find no ending" was itself the moral of Franklin's fable, and he was supported by Maurice and Ralph. Some of the other children disagreed and insisted that Franklin had not succeeded in writing a fable. Franklin wasn't sure himself what he had done and timidly agreed with both sides.

The third time Franklin read his piece to the class Alvin jumped up with one of his questions which threw the whole issue to me.

"What is a fable anyway, Mr. Kohl?"

I wasn't prepared to answer. The issue seemed too complex to discuss with the class. After all, there are no clear and unambiguous rules that establish what is or isn't a fable. I thought of the fables I had read before introducing the class to the subject. Some were animal tales and some weren't, some had explicit morals while others didn't. No single list of characteristics seemed possible to describe all and only those pieces of writing that were fables. There were many short tales like Franklin's that may or may not have been fables according to how rigidly and artificially one wished to draw boundaries between forms of written expression. I didn't want to draw the boundaries at all, yet I also didn't want to leave the children with the impression that the word "fable" had no meaning at all.

I remembered a discussion of the meaning of words in Ludwig Wittgenstein's *Philosophical Investigations* and despite Alvin's objections that I wasn't answering his question tried to do a bit of philosophy with my class.

I put the word "game" on the blackboard and asked the children to list all the games they could. At first the class was puzzled. Soon they forgot about the fable question, however, and fell to naming games—football, chess, baseball, ring-a-levio, basketball, potsy, jump rope, playing house. After we had twenty or more games listed on the blackboard I asked the class to try to make a list of all the characteristics that games had in common. Maurice suggested that all games had fields or boards, Michael suggested they involved more than one person, Neomia that they were fun for the people involved. I made a chart on the board and asked the children to think carefully about their list of characteristics and see whether it was true that all games had even one characteristic in common. They copied my chart and filled it in.

| all games | those that do | those that don't |
|---|---|---|
| have boards or fields | baseball, chess, basketball, football | playing house, jump rope, word games |
| more than one person | football, basketball, baseball, chess | solitaire, puzzles |
| are fun | baseball, etc. sometimes | baseball, etc. sometimes |
| have pieces or balls or other equipment | baseball, etc. | word games, ring-a-levio, chase |

The only thing the children tentatively agreed upon was that all games seemed to have rules. They also agreed that "rules" meant so many different things for different games that they would have to make a chart for "rules" too and look at the different ways that word could be used.

Alvin followed all of this with a puzzled expression, then commented.

"Mr. Kohl, you didn't tell me what fables are, now I don't know what games are. What are games?"

"Well, football, basketball, chess. . . ."

There were cries of "unfair" and "phoney" in the room and the children were right. I had created an example, yet not really explained it. I tried, though with little confidence that my explanation would be understood.

"We haven't found anything that all games have in common. But look at the list again. Some games have a lot in common with each other, like baseball and basketball and football. Other games don't seem to have anything much in common, like spelling games and playing house, or playing house and baseball. It's as if you start with one game, let's say baseball, and put down other games that have something in common with it. Then we take those games and put down games they are like. You can keep building and building until you get most of the games down.

                    baseball
    football                    chess              spelling games
                    cards

They all don't have one or a list of things in common, but they're like relatives. Some have more things in common with other games, some have so little in common that you're not sure if they're games or not."

Pamela volunteered.

"You mean like when Maurice chases Alvin around?"

"Exactly. It's the same with fables, some have a lot in common with each other and some, like Franklin's, have less in common with other fables."

Alvin summed up by remarking to Michael that Charles's and Thomas's fables were brothers whereas Franklin's was only a poor cousin.

I don't know how many children understood what I was trying to say. Reginald told me that he did by putting two short pieces on my desk which he described as almost fables.

*Reginald*

I had just came up from down South. And I was looking for an apartment. As I was walk by the East river, I heard someone say help me help me. I ran to were I heard the voice. And there was a man in the river, he said help me mr. I said whats your name he said, he said Bill B B B Bill King. He said But help me I said were you live at he said Lenox Terrace. What floor 2 What number 3r, B B But help me thanks by. Within 10 min I was at Lenox Terrace 2 floor 3r I knok at the door a man opened it. I said hey you don't belong here the man that owns this apartment is drowned. I know but I am the one that pushed him in. So I went back down South and stayed there.

*Reginald*          ON PLAYING AROUND

I like to play around. Sometimes I get in trouble and sometimes I don't. I like to run around a lot. Sometimes when I run around I get hurt. One day I was walking down the street and a boy with a gang wanted to fight me I ran and that made my motto He who runs live to run again.

One lesson led to another. I introduced the children to parables, essays, character sketches, short stories. Different children found different forms congenial. Some were comfortable talking about themselves or other children.

### Kathleen

The most unusual person I have ever met is Phyllis Griffen, in what way? in this way, first Phyllis would be your friend and then your enemy, some of our friend's are sometimes like that but this one is unusual she'll play with you and have fun and if you come to school looking all nice and pretty and she's not, she'll talk about you and say "Kathleen thinks she's so cute or Marie thinks she's so cute," Now for all I know that's jealousy, And that old sain still exzist's, "sticks and stones will break my bone's but words will never bother me." I still say it because I say it still exzist's. And then after that, that enemy bussiness comes structing along. And that enemy can start a big fuss and fight, but if that enemy dose'nt agree with her she won't have an enemy to agree with her, or be jealous with her, but when she dose'nt have any one to chat with and start trouble she'll bring a lot of candy to school and try to force you to ask her for some, but no I'm not stupid? and Im not brilliant but I know not to ask her, in supprise she might even say no, I'd feel inbarrished. And I would'nt be a bit supprised if she did'nt have any teeth at all!

### Reginald

The most unusual person I have ever met is Michael. Because one min he is with you and the next min he is'nt. If somthing happens he is quik to tell. When the chips are down, he doesnt want you to tell on him. And he will tell stories as quick as a rat can run to save his neck. He is somtimes sly and skeny plus tricky. And do just about anything to get a laugh. And that my friends is the most unusual person I have ever met.

### Charisse

I am sorry to say that I have never met in unusual person But I have met a very friendly person. This person is name Barbara. You have never seen her in a fight with any of her class mates. She is a friendly person. There have been times when to people in the class have a fight. She remains an both of there sides. She doesn't take one side. I have never heard her talk about anyone. She and Pam Reed are the best of friends. You can always see them playing.

Out of the many years Barbara has been in my class I have never seen her fight. She has the gitf of making friends. I hope that she will use her friendship to help people in need. In the many fights I have gotten in Barbara has always remain a friend.

A few children excelled at writing short, sometimes bitter essays and stories.

*Marie*  March 8    MAKING AND LOSING
                     FRIENDS

Whenever you make friends with someone soon or later you will have a fight with them then a day or so you're friends again it is better to lose a friend then to make because if you be with another person and your other friend see you with another person than they'll say that you aren't they friend. Soon when you go someplace else they go and talk about you next they eat up all your candy, make fun of you then later they go and call you names.

*Phyllis*  May 23

One dull day my sister and when for a walk. Soon we found our selfs in a 117 St. so we decided to visit our aunt. When we walked our aunt was selling dope and whiskey. We tried to get a way but we were caught. They tied us up an whipped us. Then they punched us in the face. They kicked us in the face, and threw us out the window. We were in the hospital for a whole month. When we got out, we found out that our mother had beat them up. One thing I forgot to say is that it was a dull day.

*Phyllis*  Feb. 8

You say hello and what's you name and name is so and so and let's play. I live at stough and stough a place, where do you live? Well you say goodbye and I don't want to be your friend anymore.

P.S. —— is located near Park Avenue and 119th Street. Since I had taken some children the length of Park Avenue, I decided to take the entire class across 119th Street as far as the Hudson River. One morning we set out from school westward across Harlem. After a leisurely hour's walk we reached

Morningside Park where the children were content to settle.
It was only ten thirty, but they wanted to have lunch and then
play. Most of them had been to the park before and liked it.
But I insisted that we cross the park and climb the stairs to
Morningside Drive. The children hesitated. They had never
been up there, were afraid they weren't supposed to be there.

I started up alone. Alvin, then Maurice and Michael followed. Grace, Pamela, Marie, then Neomia, Gail, and Desiree
came. After a while I stood with the entire class gazing down
at Harlem sweeping across to the East River.

"Mr. Kohl, look at the bell!"

After spotting the bell tower in Mount Morris Park the
children picked out the school, speculated on the location of
their houses, noticed uptown, downtown, acrosstown, the gray
sweep of New York. Then they turned away from Harlem to
confront Columbia University sitting indifferently above the
park and the Harlem community below.

One hundred and twentieth Street and Amsterdam Avenue, the School of Engineering, Teachers College. . . . The
children had no idea that Columbia University existed, though
we could see it from our classroom window. I took the children to the Teachers College cafeteria where we sat and had
lunch. Not that people didn't stare and sit uncomfortably next
to us. Marie sat down next to me and asked: "Who do they
think they are anyway, rolling their eyes at us?"

I explained to her that the people she saw were training
to become teachers. She smiled and nodded. That explained
the hostility and coldness.

After lunch we walked through the campus, visited the
chemistry museum, the school of architecture, the psychology
labs. We met many hostile academics, yet there were exciting
moments for the children. Two graduate students in psychology showed them their mice and demonstrated a few simple
experiments. A distinguished professor of genetics took a moment to show the children fruit flies and explain some elementary principles of genetics.

When we returned to school the children were exhausted
but content. Another new world had opened for them. Alvin
and Maurice were plotting a private visit to Columbia the next
day; Samuel, Thomas, and John were returning that afternoon
to the Teachers College Bookstore to buy book-covers and
souvenirs. New words were alive in the children's conversation: chemistry, architecture, genetics, hereditary, maze-learn-
ing. The children connected *psychology* with the word they
knew in connection with Cupid and Psyche. As a teacher, it
was thrilling to see them learning so spontaneously.

Over the year the creation of myths was one of the children's favorite challenges. Initially we only spoke of Greek mythology, and the children's stories were peopled by their own versions of Cyclops, Psyche, Hades, and Zeus. Maurice and Michael changed that by introducing members of the League of Justice—Superman and Wonder Woman—and movie characters such as Dracula and the Frankenstein monster into their stories. I remember Michael's *Cyclops Meets Frankenstein* in which Cyclops and the Frankenstein monster battled over the lovely Psyche, whom Michael saved at the last minute from both of them. Maurice contributed adventures of the League of Justice in which the members of the League did not always triumph.

We talked about comic books in class, and about heroes and monsters. I brought in pictures of ancient monsters and told the class of the Minotaur and the Sphinx. From the children I learned about Gorgo and Godzilla. For a while some of the children would come up to the room before nine o'clock, and we would swap tales.

I asked the children if there were any neighborhood myths or legends, and though they were reluctant to talk about them at first they began to speak of heroic villains who were "upstate" in prison but unbroken by the police, of stories they heard about beautiful women and strong, bad men who lived down south and got away with fooling and defying the white man. I encouraged the children to talk and blend past and present, to let their imaginations create mythical worlds. I also encouraged them to write and share their fantasies. In the case of a few children, and most notably Robert Jackson, the creation of myths and heroic tales became almost an obsession.

### Gail

One day a boy named Skyview was walking alone when a greek god appeared. The Greek gods name was Missile. He was a very kind man. He loved to help people who needed things. Well Skyview didn't have a home, he was lonely. When Missile appeared he said: "What can I do for you? Skyview said who are you. My name is Missile. Can I help you in any way? Why yes, if it isn't any trouble. I have no home and no money. And all of a sudden a large rich looking house appeared with maids and servants. Then a whole room full of money and jewels. Skyview was very happy. He thanked Missile and walked up the stairs of his new home. Day after day, week after week, month after month, year after year,

Skyview was happy. Then one day something happen to Skyview. He became the King of Dime. Skyview then became cruel. He made the people slave for him. He wanted power over all the lands. Skyview remembered about Missile and wanted to get all of Missiles riches. Then Missile appeared. Skyview said give me your riches or I'll kill you. Missile said no, and Skyview killed Missile. All of a sudden all the riches disappeared the maids, the servants, the money, the jewels everything. Skyview was poor again, and the people of dime had to slave no more for Skyview's power was gone. He didn't know but the riches would only stay as long as Missile was alive but if he was killed or died the riches would disappear. poor, sad SKYVIEW.

### Ralph

Once there was a smart man. He was honored by everone. Everyone was suppose to bow down to him. As a Great leader, he was very poor. He lost his richness because he was greedy for houses and land. But no body knew this. As time passed he wanted slaves. So he comanded for a slave. The Slave was very smart. Soon he found out about the king. The Slave told his friends. Soon Everyone was talking about it.

The people were mad they threw him out. Then the Slave took the leaders place. He ruled good and wisely. For the king he was put to a task of rolling rocks (huge rocks) on a mountain that erupts. The Slave set all Slaves free and gave them money and land.

### Dianne    WAR AND PEACE

This story takes place in Germany where all the war breaks out. So one day this turtle and frog were talking about it. The turtle I wonder why there is so much war! And as time as the last letter came out of his month a big bomb was heard. Everybody started to scream and shout We Want peace, we want pec—before they could finish the word it was like a miricle. A angel appeared before their eyes. And she said I will grant your wish there will be no more War! So from that day on there were peace and happiest Everyone was very happy.

### Robert

One day, my friend and I worked on a machine, it was supposed to be a brain-machine. Whatever you say to it, it answers back to you. When we finished with it, we decided

to test it. I asked it what was the longest word in the world.
And it answered, "The longest word in the world is antidistab-
lishmentariumism." It worked. But just then, two guys walked
in. "My name's Uiop, Werty Uiop." said one of them. "How
'bout selling me that machanical brain for $10,000." We hesi-
tated for a min. finally, "No." That's when we saw the loaded
shootin' irons. "Too bad you guys cannot get to live. You
could have had $10,000 in your hands." But then I had an
idea, if it's the machine they want, it's the machine they'll
get. "So you guys want the machine, eh? Give it to them,
Frank." "What? What do you mean, Robert?" "Do as I say."
So we gave them the machine. A few days later, when they
got to their country, they demonstrated it to their leader. "is
not our country the greatest among all?

And it answered back, "No. Your country stinks and so
does the leader." The leader of the country slayed the two
spies and punished his country. He made the people pay more
taxes and made it grow more powerful. As for the machine,
it was sent back to America.

Here's what the country looked like:

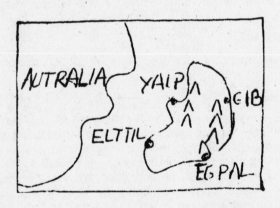

*The small Country of Llams*

Capital: Elttil
Largest City: Egral
Chief Sea Port: Gib
Chief Imports: rice, beans and gas
Chief Exports: Gold, uranium, and dairy products
Chief Trading Center: Yalp

Alvin's *Elektra* was a special case. One Saturday during the spring I took Alvin, Robert, Pamela, Carol, and a few other children to see Michael Cacoyannis's *Electra*. I had seen the film a week before and felt that it would reveal to the children more of the harshness and beauty of Greece than any photographs or words of mine. It portrayed the Electra myth with such immediacy and lack of false glamour that the passion and tragedy of the story sprang forth. I was sure the children hadn't experienced anything like it before.

On the way home from the film they were strangely subdued. Robert Jackson told me that he never thought a movie could be so serious and upsetting. Electra and her sister, their terrifying mother Clytemnestra, Orestes the good but irresolute brother, the chorus of old women waiting for vengeance and death, willing it—none of this, especially the family confrontations, was what the children imagined myth to contain.

Alvin was the most affected. He was the last child to be taken home, and as we sat in front of his house on 116th Street and Fifth Avenue talking about the film the playfulness of his questioning for once disappeared.

"Mr. Kohl, do you mean that I can do what I want with a myth? Make Orestes into any kind of man I want and write about his worries and how hard it is to have to kill someone you love in order to avenge someone else you love? I mean, it's not true, but Orestes is a little like me, only he's not. It's that the whole story, I understand it in my own way, can I write it that way too?"

That Monday Alvin began his *Elektra*, or perhaps more appropriately, his *Orestes*. He didn't get very far, he couldn't. He wanted to do more than any child and all but the rarest of adults could do. He wanted to recreate the story of Electra —of family love, murder and ambiguity—in a way that would be uniquely his. I always read Alvin's fragment of a story in awe of what he wanted it to be.

## ELEKTRA *by Alvin Lewis Curry*

### FOREWORD

This story called Elektra is of the deepest passion and the deepest hope of avengence of her father's death. Her father was called Aggememnon, Aggemomnom was the rightful ruler of Argos. (His palace was in Mycenae a city of Argos) He had been cruely slaughtered by his wife Clytemnestra and her lover Aegisthus.

Agemenon was also the head of the Greek army that laid

siege to Troy. He gathered this army after Helen, the wife of his brother Menelaus, ran off with Paris.

You will also read about the many dreadful decisions the Greek Heroes faced and sacrifices they had to make and how they went about settling these problems. This story in one way or another has something to do with the trojan war and the Greeks.

## I. HOW THE TROJAN WAR STARTED

It all started when Paris a handsome prince of Troy fell in love with Helen of Troy who was the wife of Menelaus. Paris had run off with Helen And when Menelaus heard of the news he called his soldiers together with his Brother Agamemnon. Agamemnon had went on the trip to Troy in order to conquer the Trojans and get more riches, for he was a great warrior. But Menelaus had gone only in search of his wife Helen and to get revenge on Paris for running off with her.

But before they were to sail, there was a great decision!, to be made which you will read in the next chapter

## II. THE DECISION!!!

It was a busy day in Argos especially for the men for they were loading the ship with food, weapons, and fresh water, as a matter of fact they were packing enough equipment for a long journey. As Agamemnon made a undouting statement. "Make ready to open the keeps my people for we will be back with more than enough prisoners." With a loud yell the people of troy remarked "Hail Agamemnon may he triumph o'er the Trojans," following this Agamemnon, Menelaus, and his warriors were off to the ship as they Boarded the ship a last farewell the anchor was let in and all vas well. Agamemnon had started to get comfortable Before the sailed now they were sailing a little way when unexpectingly the winds stopped blowing and the seas were mild then a voice rang out Wise King of Argos you are to make a decision between triumph or failure you are to sacrifice your youngest and best loved daughter iphigenia in exchange of triump but if you don't choose either one your people will suffer Agamemnon had a dreadful decision to make. The soldiers were talking among themselves about the situation. Agamemnon defiantly sai "it is not for you to decide you don't have to do anything but just wait I am trying to decide" Suddenly he yelled out

"My decision is "TRIUMPH" he was going to sacrifice Iphegenia in exchange for triumph. He put Iphegenia on the altar and slit her throat and gave her blood and body to Zeus.

### III. PLOTTING FOR AGAMEMNON'S DEATH

It was while Clymenestra Agamemnon's Wife who was in Argos had heard of the sacrificial to Zeus she said to herself "Now I have an excuse to kill Agamemnon. Then my lover Aegisthus and I will take over the kingdom and I will throw electra and Orestes out of the kingdom" While Clymenestra was plotting over Agamemnons death, Agamemnon was in Troy conquering the trojans not knowing what was in store for him. It was about time for the return trip to Argos. Electra had heard the news that her father, Agamemnon had gone to troy (She had just heard of the news because her mother Clymenestra made her own daughter a servant and in the palace a servant doesn't have enough time and privilege to listen to the good news) and she was overjoyed to hear the good news.

### IV. THE ASSAISINATION

It was a beautiful day in the city of Argos an exciting one for the news was all about the city that Agamemnon was on his way back to his city today. Every respectful citizen of Argos was at the pier ready to greet there long gone King, as the ship came in the whole city cried out "hail Agamemnon our wise Just King The Ship had stopped at the pier and Agamemnon was walking triumphitly off the ship and behind him were the trojan prisoners Agamemnon announced "there will be a great feast tonight, to celebrate our victory over troy so go home an make ready for the feast" he told the soldiers to "take the prisoners to the Keeps, for I shall make ready for the feast Also. Agamemnon rode to the palace, as he entered Aegisthus (who had been in the room alone with Clymenestra) hid swiftly behind the throne chair Agamemnon kissed his wife Clymenestra hello and he went to take a royal Bathe (for he hadn't had one since his voyage) Aegisthus came from behind the throne chair and said "I have a plan just give me that net and that axe Clymenestra obeyed and gave Aegisthus the axe and the net. Aegisthus slowly crept into the Bathe then threw the net over Agamemnon took the axe a cruely slaughtered him. After it had all happened Clymenestra exclaimed "That was the Best gesture you ever attempted to make my lover, Now the kingdom shall Be ours." But so happened that Electra Clymenestra's daughter had seen and heard everything that had happened the past few minutes. "I plan to tell everybody what happened But will they Believe me? As she questioned herself Doubtfully!

### V. MARRIED TO A STRANGER!

The night when the feast was going on Agamemnon did not show up but Clytemnestra did. After a long time everybody got tired of waiting for the presence of their king 2 men volunteered to go and see what keeping the King "I'll go to, wait" demanded Clymenestra as she entered the palace she sent the two men to search the rest of the rooms, while she went to search the royal Bathe. she went in knowing what she would find. She then made a false but ear piercing scream everybody came rushing to the palace (not knowing what had happened) and then she did a faking (But real in the eyes of the people) faint. One of the men looked into the Bathe to see what had happened. "Great Gods" the man exclaimed "Agamemnon is dead." dead! the men exclaimed dead! everybody said in Unison dead! There was a great mixup in the crowd everybody was rushing to see what had happened the women screamed. The men started to pray "O Gods why didst thou let such a misery to beffall us" (while all the excitement was going on Clymenestra the queen had awaken) It is not for you to question the decision of the Gods! go and get some rest my people tonite has been a night full of miseries. The people agreed and went home. Electra who had seen and heard everything said "I'll take my chances and spread the news of what I had just seen!" The next day Electra spreaded the news about Clymenestra.

One thing that particularly delighted me was Alvin's and Robert Jackson's collaboration on an unfinished alphabet book that would not be, as they put it, "phoney."

A is for Alvin, the chipmunk in class;

B is for Bill, who made his cut fast!

C. is for Clyde, the Fagit in Jeans.

D is for David; kicked out by a Queen.

E is for Edward, who lives in a can.

F is for Franky who ~~tried~~ tried to play Superman.

G is for "Goofy," who goofed up the walls.

H is for Henry, who swallowed the ball.

J is FOR IVORY WHO GOT SLAPPED ON THE BEAN

I P's FOR JANEY WHO'S MOTHER IS MEAN

K is FOR KATHY WHO FELL UP THE STAIRS

L is FOR LARRY WHO SWALLOWED CAT HAIRS

~~M is~~
M is FOR MICHEAL WHO HIT HIS HEAD

N is for NEOMIE WHO SLEEP ONDER THE BED

O is FOR OSWALD WHO SWAllOWED A
STICK

P is FOR PETER WHO'S MENTAlly Sick

Q is FOR QUEENIE WHO MADE ~~SUICIDE~~
SUICIDE

R is FOR Richard WHO HITCHHIKED
A RIDE

S IS FOR STUPID WHO SLEPT UNDER A
CAR!

I READ ALL of the children's papers, commented on them and forgot about marks. Some children wrote beautiful stories and never grasped what a fable was all about. Others could turn an indifferent story into a subtle joke but were thoroughly unable to go beyond them. At one time or another all of the children tried some form of writing. I didn't insist that *everyone always* work, realizing by then that I had no right as a teacher and a person to demand of the children what I couldn't demand of myself. Before each writing lesson I vowed to do the assignment myself. Often I spent evenings devising complex means of avoiding or "forgetting" my vow. At other times I wrote bad fables and bland poetry though I surprised myself with several parables that still please me. I drew a total blank when I tried to put a simple joke down in writing. These experiences sobered me; the children's struggle with language was my own and therefore it was easy not to force them to write things that embarrassed them, or that might lead them to reject writing altogether because they couldn't use one particular form of written expression. Teachers ought to attempt to do the writing assignments they give before deciding upon criteria to judge children's efforts. What would happen to the grading of children's poetry if teachers used examples of their own work instead of Robert Frost or Walt Whitman as models for grading?

These class writing lessons were completely independent of the books some of the children were working upon individually. I didn't tie them together, but let the children apply whatever they learned in the group lessons in any ways they felt relevant to their personal writing. That was not my original inclination. I tried to point out some of the things "we" learned in writing fables to Robert Jackson during one of the first times he let me see *Journey Through Time and Space*. He was offended and retreated—I wasn't responding to his work but preaching. More, I forgot that "we" didn't learn a particular series of listable facts or definite skills. We responded in many different ways and learned many different things when we attempted to write fables. It is very hard to escape the we-fact model of elementary education—"we" meaning the whole class and usually excluding the teacher

136

who says "we" study a lesson, and then can demonstrate what we learned by listing it. Expressive writing and the concomitant explorations of self and the world can just not be listed.

As the writing accumulated in the class and the walls of the room flowered with the children's work, the uneasy pride and generous greed characteristic of many writers developed. The children wanted a larger audience; they wanted to share their work and at the same time receive the praise they felt it deserved and confront the criticism they feared it would evoke. Several children suggested independently that the class create a newspaper or magazine. I think it was in late November that I gathered all the journals and magazines in my apartment and brought them to class. For the first time the children saw *Time, Life, Dissent, i.e., etc.,* and after a while the class fell to discussing titles for their own magazines. There was no need to bother with a discussion on whether or not there would be one.

As I remember, the children were fascinated with the simplicity of magazine titles, something I hadn't thought of myself until the children pointed it out. The idea that abbreviations such as *i.e.* and *etc.* could be used made the process of finding titles easy. If *Life* could be used so could *Death*; *Look* led to *See, Find, Search*; *Time* easily led the children to suggest *Night, Work,* and *Second.*

Robert Jackson suggested *et al, Children,* and *Why.*

Alvin countered with *Because, Often,* and *Maybe.*

Barbara offered *And,* and the class dropped their other words and rhapsodized on its advantages.

"*And* could be used on posters, Robert could draw people and have them say '*And.*' "

"Everyone will be puzzled at what we mean."

"It's cool, it doesn't commit us, we can put anything in it. Last year we had to use *The 5-1 Gazette.* Ugh. . . ."

At least that is the way I remembered it. Last week I asked Pamela whether she remembered how we got the name *And,* and she smiled and told my wife.

"Judy, we only did it to humor him. He liked silly names."

Recently I've shown some of the children things they'd written, and they had forgotten them. How much truth is there in Pamela's memories and how much distortion and romanticization in mine? I honestly don't know. The children's writings exist; they are repeatable and reproducible. The experiences that gave rise to this literature are more elusive. I perceived them from my teacher's desk and remember them now with a pen in my hand. In support of my effort to reach as much of the truth of my classroom as I can, the best witness I can call is Alvin—not Alvin today who remembers very little of 6-1, has no time for memories in the burden and torture of his present. Rather I have to call on Alvin the author, whose *The Boy in the Slums* has shown me something of myself and the class through the sensitive alien eyes of a child.

# THE BOY IN THE SLUMS:

### A Story of Modern Life in "Uptown" New York, with Comments, Passions and a Few DIRECT Questions

### FOREWORD

This story is about a boy namely me, who lives in a apartment in and around the slum area. I feel that other people should be interested in what I have to say and just like me, *try* to do something about it, either by literal or diatribe means. This Book is only to be read by men and women boys and girls who feel deeply serious about segrigation and feel that this is no joke. Especially when you are younger you have a better oppunity to speak about and be willing to work for these problems of the slums. Let me ask you some personal questions that may have to do with this book!!!

1. Do you live in the slums?
2. How do you think you would feel if you did?
3. Would you rather be rich have mades and servants to take care of you while your mother is away to dinners, nite-clubs and business trips? Or would you rather be poor and your mother'd be home to *Love* and take care of you?

Before I wrote the last question down I made sure that at least *I* knew the answer I had a decision to make also because my mother asked that same question just a few days ago and take it from me its not easy to answer a question like that But if jist by mere curiosity you would like to know my answer to this question jist open the pages of this Book and read to your hearts content And do me a favor (just as a friend) tell other people about this Book and *maybe* they may be encouraged to read this Book. (Oh by the way all through this book a word will be underlined and if by any chance you want to know what this word means just look it up in the Back of this Book it is called: "Alvin's Slang Dictionary").

## I. A INTRODUCTION TO MY MOTHER

I am dreaming and crying in my sleep. I am dreaming because I have nothing better to do and crying because I am dreaming About a problem I had in school, you see I promise myself I'll be good and try to learn more; but everytime I come into the classroom (in my dream) my teacher right then and there starts to pick on me Alvin this or Alvin that. So I say to myself "enought is to much everyday the same old problem" why that's enough even to make a laughing hyena cry, so I can imagine quite clearly why thats a good enough reason to cry. (wouldn't you if you were in my situation?). Just as I was about to cry in my sleep for the second time unexpectly a hand hit me right on my rear end (I knew it was a hand because I had felt this more than once) of course I woke up and immediately knew that it was time for my brother and my sisters and me to get ready to go to school. My youngest sisters name is Turia she is 3 years next comes Patsy she is 8 years old my next sister's name is Linda She is 9 years old then comes my Brother who's name is Gregory he is 10 years then comes me Alvin I am 11 years then comes my next sister Sharon she is 12 years going on thirteen And last But not least my oldest sister who's name is Brenda she is 14. I know you're not interested in my private life but I'll fill you in a little way just to have something interesting to say. The first thing I have to do is head straight for the *Bathe* room—P.S. (By the way the word *Bathe* is just a fancy word I picked up from my teacher "Mr. Herbert Ralph Kohl." You know I'll let you in on a little secret. Mr. Kohl is kind of fancy himself. The reason why I'm telling you this is because my teacher told me to express myself to the *fullest extent.* (thats another fancy word I learned from my teacher)—and the first thing I do in the Bathe room is to wash my face and comb my hair, while my mother is ironing my shirt and pants. Oh by the way my mothers name is Mrs. Helen Curry (You can call her *ma* or Mrs. Helen cause that what I always call her and she doesn't get mad either). The next thing I do is eat my breakfast which consists of 2 or 3 jelly sandwiches and a glass of water or if I'm lucky I'll have a bowl of cereal with *can milk.* At this time it should by 8:30 time to go to school. PS 79 here I come I say as I start out of the door to my building. As I walk along to school which is within walking distance from my house I begin to think of things that could but then again couldn't happen. For example: Maybe someday I'll be a scientist or a big businessman or maybe even a engineer or then again the President of the United States or maybe even the mayor. As long as it is somebody important. You see! some people are lucky enought to be born important but not me I'll have to work my way up to what I want to be if I'm even lucky enought to get that far up as a matter of fact I'll even be lucky if I get pass the sixth Grade the way things are going now. If you ever get into a situation similar to mine take my advise don't give up, you have to work for your goal, don't worry you'll never be alone in your problems other people just like you are sharing your same problems. P.S. This is my own personel opinion of the situation.

I feel I'll have to close this chapter now for I am digging into my long buried problems which you probably wouldn't Be interested in anyhow. But do me a favor read on to the next chapter!

"Theres no time like the Present so read the next chapter *now.*

## 2. "A AVERAGE DAY IN SCHOOL"

The first thing you have to do in my school is to get on the line that forms outside of the school. You see you have to get on this line in order to get into the school or else you'll have to stay outside or play *hookie* but if by chance you don't feel like playing hookie all you have to do is walk right in and get a *late pass.* After you go throgh the process of getting into my school you hafta go into the yard and then you can talk all you want to but the Bad thing about it is that you can't run around play or box all you can do is just stand around and *talk to each other just like little old ladies.* (thats what my teacher always says when he gets mad cause we talk to much). And then we have to be quite when the Bell rings which goes *Boing* but this is kinda silly cause they ring 3 bells instead of one, just for extra silence extra silence I guess. Next after the bells ring we have to walk 6 flights of stairs in order to get to the third floor. When we get to the third floor we hafta walk down almost to the end of the hall to room 330 class 6-1 Teacher Mr. Kohl (he tells <u>corny</u> jokes) (thats what it says on the door of my classroom) PS. By the way Mr. —— is my honorable Principal of my school. When we get into the fancy new classroom which is already beginning to look like <u>Beanschool</u> —— we hang up our coats on to our assigned hooks and then my teacher puts the presession on the board then we have to sit down and you don't have to do the pre-session only if you're writing a book just like I'm doing now (thats why I don't have to do the Presession) then we do reading, music, practice the no play then we go to lunch which consists of meat, vegetables, milk, Bread and Butter and dessert next we go outside and play until its time to go back in we get on line march in the Bell rings we march upstairs (the reason why we march so much is because we are not allowed to run up the stairs) and walk down the hall to room 330 hang up our coats sit down talk awhile and then we have to do arithmetic, science, composition and park.

So as you can see this is a plain normal day in school you are invited to visit my school and make you're own opinion of it this invitation still holds the school is located.

THE CHILDREN created *And*. They chose an editorial board, chose the selections to be published, and put them on rexograph paper—going through at least a dozen master sheets for every page that passed their own scrutiny. Robert drew posters, enticing pictures of famous men declaiming . . . *And*. Dennis and Thomas commandeered the rexograph machine while Alvin and Leverne managed to slip copies of Robert's posters into teachers' mailboxes, under doors, even onto the principal's desk.

...And

DR. KILDARE and BEN CASEY SAYS...

...And

After several weeks' work the girls presented the finished masters. Dennis and Thomas ran off five hundred copies and then the class spent a chaotic day attempting to collate the pages. They ended up with two hundred copies for distribution and a monumental cleaning job which they did with great joy.

# ...And!

**THE CLASS NEWSPAPER** that tells you more things in the class than any other magazine! It gives you more enjoyment than any other magazine! This magazine gives you more than The Children's Tribune! This magazine tells you more than The 401 Gazette! So remember, get the "...And."

PRES. KENNEDY SAYS...

And ...

*by Robert Jackson*

## THE STORY OF MYTHOLOGY

Mythology was sometimes believed in a few hundred years ago in Greece, Rome, China, Egypt, and even in America, when the Indians told them. Other places too. Some legends were told about places, people, animals, and plants. Or some were told about the start, or gods. Some myths were told because some people didn't know the outside-world, some didn't know what some things were, and told what they thought they were. Mythology is the study of legends, and tales. Some mythologists study some of the Greek and Roman myths, because the Greeks and Romans are some of the best story tellers of the world. When they look at the stars, they get ideas from them. Like for instance, the sun comes up every morning. They think of it as a man in a golden chariot riding in the sky. His name is Apollo, the god of the sun, music, and poetry. Another one, this time, a planet. Let's pick pluto. Since pluto is so far away, they would make this, "Pluto, the god of the underworld." That's how their ideas are. Anyone can think of a myth. A baby, smart person, and a dumb kid.

**PAN**
The half-man, half-goat Greek god who brought trouble all over the world wherever he went.

**ATLAS**
The mighty giant according to the Greeks, he held up the earth.

**PERSEUS BEHEADING MEDUSA**
With Mercury's help, Perseus cut off the head of Medusa.

**MARS**
The fierce god of war.

**VENUS**
The goddess of love and beauty.

**MERCURY**
The speedy messenger of the gods, also a symbol of medicene, and telegraph stations.

**APOLLO**
The god of music, and the sun.

**DIANA**
The maiden goddess of the chase of the moon.

## OH WHAT A DAY

*By Neomia Cook*

ONE day Gail, Brenda, Gloria, and I were walking down
Madison Ave. when suddenly a man came running toward us
with a gun in his hand. We became so scared that we all ran
in directions. Then once again we met each other and when
we turned around to go back home we said to the man, Please
don't shoot' Please don't shoot!" But is was to late; the man
was getting ready to shoot us when suddenly I heard a shot
and the man had dropped dead. We looked around to see
where the shot came from, and who do you think it was?
. . . . . . , our teacher Mr. Kohl 'We said to Mr. Kohl, 'Did
you shoot that man. The teacher said, "Yes I did". We became so surprised that we said, "Mr. Kohl you are a hero".
Mr. Kohl said, Oh it was nothing". But we knew he was proud
of himself. (DON'T YOU).

POEM:

### The Junkies

When they are
in the street
they pass it
along to each
other but when
they see the
police they would
run some would
just stand still
and be beat
so pity fųl
that they want
to cry

*Marie Ford*

## CLASS OPINIONS ON INTEGRATION

### Barbara

I think we sould have some integration but not to much.
We should have intergrated schools so children of other races
could learn and see the way other people work and play and
act.

If we have intergration we will learn more. We can use
their ideas and they can use ours.

But we shouldn't have to much. Such as over crowding
a school just to show the people of a race that you aren't
prejudice.

I think sometimes people don't really like that race of
people so much that they have to over crowd a school. It's
because they want you to think it, and praise them.

### By Thomas S.

I think that it should integration becuse every body
blood is the same Just because somebody skin is white an
another person skin is black that donot mean that they have
fight, because they blood is the same people can not change
the color of they skin

### By Sonia Newton

I don't think we need any integration, because the white
people in Mississippi doesn't act right to be alive. Just like for

James Merdith. He went to the University of Mississippi to get a nice education so that he could support his family and what do he get?

He got bombs thrown at him, He was threatened, and was shot at. He had just as much right as anyone to get a good education. It really doesn't matter on the color. I think negro and white children should go to the same school and live in the same block. But I don't like to see negro lady marrying a white man it don't look so good. And I don't like a white man with a negro girl that don't look so good either. White children and negro children could do anything the same. I think we should have more integration but not to much they are a little bit integration in this school in other schools there should be more integration to in our class there should be more integration we have more colored than white in ever place there should be a little integration. There shouldn't be colored people in one place and white people in another. White people and colored people should get alone together.

### Reginald Potter

I think people should marry who they want to marry. Because they are the one who have to stay with one another. And if this keeps up there might be another war between the states. Color don't make any difference the white man is wash off with white dirt and the colored man is washed off with black dirt and we all have to stick together.

### Sylvia Burwell

I think the white people should stop taking advantage of the color people before they get punched in the face.

# THE DIAMOND THEFT MYSTERY

TWO DAYS AFTER *And* had been distributed to the teachers and administration, and had been read and praised by some of the children's parents we got a visit from Mary Bonnett, a big, smiling yet tough Negro teacher who considered herself the children's truest mother but who had the unenviable position of translating the principal's feelings into words the children understood. She entered the room smiling, a copy of *And* and another class newspaper in her hand. The children quickly took their seats and snapped to attention—Mrs. Bonnett always commanded attention, but this time the children were even more alert—they cared what she thought of their work.

"I just read your magazine. It was really interesting, children. Robert Jackson, you really draw beautifully, only Robert, why do you draw so much violence—child, your imagination needs to rest. Children, I don't understand why you talk of so much fighting and stabbing. You can't possibly know about that. Tell me now, who knows what a junkie is? See, I told you no one knows. Newspapers and magazines aren't for that type of nonsense. Now look at this sheet, imagine it was put out by the fifth grade. Listen to this, you know how to do better.

*"Shop With Mom*

"I love to shop with mom
And talk to the friendly grocer,
And help her make the list
Seems to make us closer."

The children slumped into their seats, demoralized.

Then she gave me a copy of *The 5-1 Gazette*, flawlessly typed and edited (by the teacher, it turned out), and explained that there was no reason my class couldn't do that.

Fifteen minutes later the assistant principal made his first visit of the year and informed me that he would teach a lesson on proofreading the next day. It was hard to tell whether the children were more depressed than I was.

The proofreading lesson destroyed the whole spontaneity of the venture, and I was ready to give up *And* altogether.

The children were much stronger. At the end of the week they decided that there would be another issue no matter what anyone said, only this time they wouldn't share it with the rest of the school. The second issue came out for our Christmas party.

THE CLASS NEWSPAPER

SANTA SAYS...
Merry Christmas

## THE EMPEROR OF ICE CREAM

*By Barbara*

Once upon a time there was an emperor, and he said, "The only emperor is the emperor of ice cream." Everyone knew that wasn't true, but they were Afraid to say anything. One day a man came up to him and said, "I'm the emperor of ice cream." When the emperor heard this he said: "I am the emperor of ice cream." They started to Argue. There was a great war. The two emperors fought Fiercly. THEE Emperor of ice cream won. The emperor smiled and said, "The only emperor is the emperor of ice cream

### POETRY

### SCHOOL

Some people think school is a mess,
    With science, spelling and math.
    Social studies, reading, geography,
    music, some English, and maps.
Teacher after teacher after teacher
    after teacher comes in day
    After day; day after day, units
    of units of units of things to do

in all kinds of ways. You get Homework
today and homework tomorrow—you get
homework every day! Now don't you think
I'm complaining, these are complaints
some people make! But I like
school, it's scintilate. It's harsh,
it's miserable, it's *fun*." Now I'm
not complaining I might be the
only one under the sun!

*By Grace*

## THE CHINA DOLLS

The china dolls sit on the dresser
day and night.
Standing very still and looking very bright.
One time during the night they had a very
fussing fight. The next morning they were
gone, but I still saw pieces torn and torn.

*by Pamela Reed*

If we could be changed into anything we wanted:

## A COLLECTION OF CLASS RESPONSES

### By Barbara

When I was a baby I was transformed from a baby to a
child, from a child to a woman.

The person that is exactly like me is me, myself, and I.
And if I must say so myself she is a very nice girl indeed.

### by Neomia

(I think) before I became what I am now I was an ugly
witch. I would treat people meanly. I would burn down their
houses, kidnap their children, and starve them to death. I
would never let them buy a new outfit or a new pair of pants.

Then one day I got tired of treating people so meanly. I
finally went to a magician. I told him my troubles and he
studied them over for a minute or so and then he said "Would
you like me to transform you into something you'd really like
to be.

I thought it over for a few minutes than I said "yes". So
the very next day he transformed me into an eleven year old
girl and from this day until march 13th I'll be an eleven year
old girl.

*by Grace*

> The thing that I was transformed
> from it's plain for you to know;
> I was transformed from an
> evil monkey, units of decades ago.
> You see I used to roam
> around being mean to bad;
> I used to roam around and
> make happy people sad.
> Now that you've heard my
> transformation, It's not easy to know
> I'm the same,
> I'm not an evil "*monkey*"
> just evil just the same.

*By Maurice*

I was transformed from a poor little infant into a nice boy, and as I grew I was transformed into a magnificent extraordinary deceiving nuisance to the world. Now I'm still the same old nuisance I ever was.

One day, when I found the man that changed me ino a nuisance, "pow" right in the kisser, and then he might just turn me back into my magnificent self, that is, if he ever recovers from the blow I gave him.

*BY Dianne*

I was transformed from a baby to a child from a child to a schoolgirl. If I could be changed again I rather be a fairy. So if I do good deeds or anything that's nice. And if I don't want any body to know I could pop outer sight.

I WISH   *by Ralph*

I wish I was ⅓ of an inch tall. Inside my apartment there would be a tiny, tiny micropolis. There I would have a small buildings like a real city. I would have small cars for myself, horses and schoolsets etc. My house would have small televisions by the dozens. When a movie comes I'd have my own theater. When it's time for school I'll send a robot in my place. I'll give him a good smart brain so that he'll know everything. Then I'll always get a hundred!

# RANDOLPH'S NAVY

OUR WORK was interrupted in February by what should have been a significant and joyous event—a new school P.S. —— opened and we moved into the new building.

The new school was built to replace P.S. ——; after years of agitation and aggravation, after innumerable construction delays and false openings, the kids could finally move out of what they called the bean school (a reference to the hastily warmed and unimaginatively conceived lunches of welfare beans and white bread that are served in schools without kitchens). A kitchen wasn't all that 103 lacked. There was no gym (we went to Mount Morris Park and mingled with the dropouts, the junkies, and the winos two days a week for physical education), no auditorium, no labs, no adequate toilet facilities, no heat . . . there is no use reciting all the building lacked. Robert Jackson summarized it perfectly well:

## MY SCHOOL

I hate this little bean school,
It is so stink and wet;
It can't afford no plumbing,
That I can bet you yet!

I said the move *should* have been joyous. Unfortunately even that was denied the children. P.S. —— had eighteen hundred pupils whereas the new school had been built according to the Board of Education's notion of the ideal size for an urban school—twelve hundred pupils. Six hundred children had to be left behind in the old building. The children could not be happy for their brothers and sisters who were left behind in the old school. It is only now as I'm writing this book, over four years later, that P.S. —— had finally been closed—four years and how many children going to school demoralized, confused, sharing a condemned half-empty building with whomever wandered in from the streets in search of a roof.

It was more pleasant in the new school. The classroom was more spacious, there were seats for everyone, and blackboards. But essentially we transferred the work we were doing in an old impossible place to a new more comfortable one. The building was new; the school wasn't. There were no new teachers, no new equipment in the school. Within a few weeks the chaos and disorder of the old school was reconstituted in the new one. The administration disappeared into new nooks and crannies, children roamed the halls teacherless, discipline-less—essentially schoolless. And there was a problem that we didn't have before. Up to that time all of the children had shared the same miserable school environment. Now the third and fourth grades were abandoned to it. Windows in the new school were broken; in many other subtle and not so subtle ways the younger children expressed their anger, despair, and feelings of rejection. The older children in the new school had their joy tainted with guilt. The children in my class asked me to do something about the problem, to change things, speak to the principal. I could only laugh sadly and confess my im-potence. The system, I had to tell them, it was the system of which I was an insignificant and powerless part that had to be changed. My choice was to remain within the system and work with the children, or leave and try to change it from without. I stayed, though now I am convinced that that system, which masquerades as educational but in Harlem produces no educa-tion except in bitterness, rejection, and failure, can only be changed from without.

I RESERVED the weekly spelling and vocabulary tests for one o'clock on Friday. They were usually over by two and so was the school week. We were all weary; there was no point in trying to teach when I didn't care to and the children didn't care to learn. I remembered my elementary school teachers who held us tightly under their control until one second after three Friday afternoon as if a slight letup at the end of the week would sweep away their authority altogether. I couldn't do that. From two to three on Friday the children wandered about the room gossiping, listening to music, playing games, cleaning up for the weekend. I packed my briefcase or chatted with a few children.

On one of these Fridays several girls were sitting by the window looking down into the street and sounding on people passing by.

"Look at that nappy old thing. Who does she think she is?"

"It rains every time she leaves her house."

Then they noticed Judy sitting in my car, waiting for the school day to end. Grace and Carol recognized her and came screaming up to me.

"Mr. Kohl, Mr. Kohl, can we?"

"Can we go down and get her?"

Before I even realized what they were talking about they had bolted out of the room. Five minutes later they returned with Judy. The boys paid no attention to her, but the girls crowded around and showed her their work or told stories— about some pretty teacher she ought to worry about or a day I lost control.

Marie and Grace became particularly attached to Judy and let me know how good they felt she was for me. Marie prodded me, pushed me. She believed in marriage though her parents were not together and her sister had had unhappy experiences. She was quiet and somewhat withdrawn in class. Her junkie poem and several other little pieces she wrote showed how compassionate she was, but her manner hid it. Only outside, in Mount Morris Park, would she occasionally open up. The rest of the class would be scattered about playing basketball, jumping rope, or just running. She would come up to me and speak seriously of her life, her fear of leaving her apartment even to walk to school, her hatred of filth and need for privacy. She often spoke with the wisdom and resignation of an old woman who has seen too much misery during her life. Then she would turn silly and be a child again. When I decided to get married, it was Marie I told first. She put her arm around me.

"Mr. Kohl, it's good for you and for us."

I had been nervous and anxious but something in her tone made me accept her words.

It was quite natural that a month later Marie conceived and planned a surprise wedding party for Judy and me. Word of our engagement had spread through the class, but the children were shy and mistrustful about it. I'm not sure they believed I would go through with it.

The wedding was scheduled for Friday afternoon, March 22. I went to school that morning and Judy and her parents were going to pick me up at noon. The children had gone to the assistant principal the day before and persuaded him to have me out of the room at ten o'clock. Their parents made cakes and cookies. The boys somehow hustled up enough money to buy soda, candy, potato chips—a lavish banquet as the children conceived it.

When I returned my classroom was transformed. Scrawled across the blackboard was "Yeah for Mr. Kohl and Miss Judy." Streamers hung from the lights and the tables were pushed together. On the middle of the table was a wedding cake. I entered and was greeted by awkward silence. I became self-conscious and blushed, blurted out a thank you, and tried to escape to the hall. Alvin and Sam blocked the way. Marie brought me a piece of cake and mercifully someone turned on the phonograph.

Judy arrived at eleven thirty and the children rushed down to the car to greet her. Only Alvin stayed behind with me. I packed my briefcase quickly and started to leave.

"You're coming back Monday, aren't you?"

I looked at him. He was genuinely scared, not that he would be hit as he feared the first day we met, but now that he and the class would be abandoned.

On Monday many of the children arrived earlier than usual and waited for me at the front door. Alvin explained that they just wanted to be sure that I was coming back.

Once they were settled in the new school the children took up their writing again. Sonia and Anastasia, the quietest girls in the class, asked me for binders. Anastasia was older than the other children and more serious. She had arrived from Panama during September and was put into the sixth grade instead of high school because she spoke no English. This didn't anger her; on the contrary, she set out to master the language and by March could read and write English almost as well as the rest of the children. She listened intently in class, did every assignment, was never absent but never spoke. The other children respected her but she was too old and too remote for them. Only Sonia became her friend, and they worked quietly together in the back of the room.

Sonia was shy and withdrawn in school but quite explosive after three o'clock. The children talked of her fights and wrath, but I never saw any of it in the classroom. Her mother visited the class one day and she looked younger than her daughter to me. When I told her that she laughed; she had five other children. Then she told me about Barbados where she had come from and the books she used to read and love. She liked the classroom, had read *Mary Jane* when Sonia took it home, but wondered why we didn't have any of the Bobbsey Twins and Nancy Drew books. I would have laughed snobbishly only she was so serious. The books had meant something to her and perhaps could be meaningful to some of the children. I promised to get the series for the class and presented some of the books the next week.

At first Sonia and Anastasia devoured the books, but after close to a dozen they tired of eternal success and partial danger. They started writing themselves and produced their own girls' books under the general series title of Girls' Mystery Series. Anastasia wrote *The Mysterious Box*; Sonia wrote *The Mystery of the Stolen Ring* and *Don't Treat Me Like a Child*.

*Don't Treat Me Like a Child* is the one Sonia let me have.

# Don't Treat Me Like a Child

*by Sonia*

## I   LONELINESS

One day this girl named Gwendolyn said to her mother "Mother an so lonely I don't have on one to play with." "Go out side and play with Karen." "I went over to her house earlier, but she said she couldn't come out because she had to mind her little sister. Every girl in this block has a little sister but me, Mom could you get me a sister?" "I have to talk it over with your father first and it wouldn't be easy."

Two days later Gwen came to her father and said, "Daddy could you play this game with me?" "Not now Gwen am busy." "But just this one game." "AM BUSY". "Mommy could you play this game with me?" "Not now honey am cooking". Gwen went out she told her mother she was going to Beth Moon's house on her way there she seen Barbie and Marie riding their bicycles and she said, "I wish I had a sister of my own to play with," when she was on Karen's block she seen Beverly and Dorothy who were twins.

She knocked on Karen's door. Karen invited Gwen in and then Karen said, "Gwen come see my baby sister." "Oh

166

she's beautiful, what's her name?" "Her name's Audrey, my mother named her after my aunt." "My mother said, she'll try to get a sister for me, but it seems like I will never have a sister." "Well am glad I have a sister." "I have to go now I told my mother I'll be back at 3:00 and its 3:30, bye." CRASH "Gwen what happened?" "I fell over this wooden box, well bye again." "Gwen did you and Karen have a fight?" "No mom I fell over a wooden box." "Go upstairs and clean yourself up, you an mess and when you come down your father and I will like to talk to you." when gwendolyn came downstairs she sat in her favorite rocking chair and her parents did the same, her father said, "Honey we know how much you want a sister, but it'll take time."

"Do you understand what your father means?" "Yes mom" "We'll try to get you a sister in two weeks or maybe in a month, that is all we wanted to talk to you about. You can go play now." "Mom why do it take so long to get me a sister, all the girls around here have a sister? Mom can't I find a sister myself." "No you're too young, now go play." "With whom I don't even have a dog?" Then Gwendolyn ran upstairs crying. "We have to do something about that child." "I'm going down to the orphanage." "Do you remember that little girl we saw at the orphanage yesterday, she's so sweet." "Which one do you mean Alice?" "That little girl that was giving us the candy." "Oh yes she'll be just right for Gwen." "She'll be coming out of that orphanage in two days." "Then why did you tell Gwen it would take a month." "I wanted to surprise her, lets not say another word, she might hear us." "I have to say more, suppose they don't get along." "Oh Anthony you could say the silliest things." "Ok, don't say I didn't warn you" "Anthony Gwen wanted a sister for years, they'll be ok."

Ding Dong

"Honey would you answer the door?" "It's for you dear, it's Mrs. Hall from the orphanage." "Send her right in, I'll be out in a second." The orphange lady said, "Hello Mrs Green, I'm Mrs. Hall." "Glad to meet you this is my husband Anthony." "Would you have a seat." "Thank you, you could pick up Gladys in two days, of course you could change her name. We will be expecting you Wednesday at ten, good bye." "Did you hear that Anthony, I'll name her, let me see what's a good name for her, let me see. Anthony help me think. I have to find a name to put on the paper."

"I have a name." "What?" "Sally" "No" "Carol" "Its

good but no" "How about Vanessa" "Yes that's a good name.
I'll call her Vanessa and we can call her Van." "Mommy
who are you going to name Vanessa and call Van?" "Nobody
a friend of mine is in the hospital, and she doesn't know a
what to name her baby. So your father and I think Vanessa
is a good name." "I wish I had a sister named Vanessa."
"Maybe you will, don't give up hope. Gwen its eight start
getting ready for bed." "Good night Mom, night Dad." "Night
Gwen." "Night Honey."

That night the house was quite, about four Gwen started
screaming, her mother and father ran in the room. They
asked her what was the matter and this what she said.

## II  TROUBLE

"I dreamed I had a sister and she started trouble, and
one day when we grew up she stuck a knife in my stomach
and in my back." "Go back to sleep now." At eight everybody woke up then Gwen's mother said, "Tomorrow when
I have to pick up that child from the orphanage. Gwen is
ten and Vanessa is ten, they'll get along together." "What
are we having for breakfast dear?" "Pancakes, eggs, bacon,
and other things." "I wonder when Gwen's coming down to
eat." "Oh here she comes now." "Gwen I told you to put
on that orange dress, not this pink one." "I'm not putting on
the orange one because I want to put on the orange one
tomorrow, to go with you and Dad." "We're going to see
that friend in the hospital." "Well can't you take me?" "No
it's private and stop asking so many questions."

"Am sorry Dad." "May I ask one more question?" "Why
yes" "What's this friends name?" "Mrs. Mason she is a
friend of Karen's mother." "Oh I'm going in the park with
Karen, and Beth, I'll be back in a little while." When Karen,
Beth, and Gwen were in the park Gwen asked Karen, "Karen
does you mother know a lady named Mrs. Mason?" "I don't
know, I'll have to ask my mother first." "Karen, Gwen I
have three swings." "Lets go" Beth, Karen, and Gwen had
icecream, they played in the sand, and played a lot of
games. Then all of the girls went home. When Karen got
home she said, "Hello mommy, do you have a lady friend
by the name of Mason." "No we just moved here a month
ago, I hardly know anybody." "Thats all I wanted to know."

Right away Karen called Gwendolyn and said, "My
mother said, she doesn't know anyone by the name of Mason."

"My mother told me she was a friend of your mother's."
"Maybe she was hiding from you, and don't tell her I told
you." "ok bye." "Gwen who were you talking to so long?"
"Karen." "Start getting ready for bed, it's past your bed
time." "Night Everybody." Back at Karen's house, Karen's
mother said, "Who were you talking to on the phone? Don't
you know you run up the phone bill". "Am sorry." "Sorry
nothing, get to bed." The next morning when Gwen and her
parents woke up she said, "Could I go with you today." "No,
for the last time, no." "If you stay home we'll bring you
back a surprise." "okay" "When Gwen's parents went out
she called Karen and said, "It's six and my mother and
father aren't home, I think they are getting me a sister." "I
have to hang up my mother is coming, and I can't use the
phone for a week, bye." "I wonder when Mom and Dad
are coming home." Then Gwen heard a knock on the door,
she answered it and saw her father, her mother and a girl
her size. Her mother said, "Gwen this Vanessa Green she is
your new sister." "Hello Vanessa." "Hello Gwen". "My real
name is Gwendolyn, but people call me Gwen, I could call
you Van." "You girls have a lot to talk about so start getting ready for bed, and you'll talk tomorrow." "When
Vanessa was in bed Gwen's mother called her in the kitchen
and said, "Gwen, Vanessa was in an orphanage, I want you
to treat her like a real sister. Now you can go to bed." "Night
Mom." Before Gwen went to bed she put her favorite Doll
in Van's bed, so Van could have a doll of her own.

Gwens mother said to Anthony, "I think they'll get
along just fine, you'll see." "I think so but not in a way."
"What do you mean?" "I'll tell you tomorrow, I'm sleepy,
night." The next morning when Gwen woke up she saw the
doll she gave Van on the floor with the head off. Gwen
started because if she knew it she would have kept it. Van
was downstairs eating her breakfast. When Gwen went downstairs she said, "Good morning, everybody." Gwen's parents
were outside on the porch and the two girls were alone so
Gwen said, "When is your birthday?" "My birthday is November 19, 1953." "My birthday is tomorrow, I'm going to
let all my friends see you." "Where are you going to get a
fork? Sit down I'll get it for you." "Could I do the dishes?"
"No I'll do them, you sit down." Then Gwen's mother called
Gwen and said, "I've been up in your room and I saw your
cinderella doll's head off." "Oh I slept on it last night and it
came off." "Are you sure?" "Yes I'm sure." "Well I'll let

your father fix it, and what's todays date?" "I'm taking Van
out to all my friends, bye."

When Van and Gwen went out, Gwen introduced Van
to Karen and to Beth. Gwen told Van to wait for her outside
until she went in the store. By the time Gwen came out of
the store Van was gone. Gwen said, "Where did that girl
go?" Then Gwen ran over to Karen's house she said, "Did
you see my sister Vanessa?" "Yes, when I asked her were
she was going she yelled in my face and said she was going
home." Vanessa went home and when Gwen's mother saw
Van come in alone she said, "Where's Gwen?" "She is playing with her friends, she told me to come home because I
wasn't wanted." "WHAT, wait until she get home, you can
go to your room."

When Gwen came home she said, "Mom did Vanessa
come home?" "Why do you ask?" "Because after I introduced
Van to three of my friends I went to a store and by the time
I came out she was gone. Then I went to Karen's house she
told me she seen Van and when she asked Van where she
was going she yelled in her face and said she was going
home. Ma Ma is Van here?" "Yes but Van told me you told
her to go home because she wasn't wanted." "That's not true,
do you believe her story?" "Yes and your Father does too."
"Mother I'm going over to Karen's." When Gwen reached
Karen's house she told Karen, "My Mother and Father believed everything Van said they don't believe me anymore.
Van is always telling fibs on me, and my Mom and Dad
believe it. If I don't talk to her she'll tell Mom and Mom
will yell at me. "That's a bad sister you have Van real bad."
Gwen went home and went right to her Father and said,
"Daddy do you believe Van's stories?" "No I think she's a
bad sister but we have her and it wouldn't be nice to take her
back to the orphanage." "I wish I was in an orphanage for
the way Mom and Van treat me." "Don' talk like that tonight at dinner table and have a talk with your Mother and
Vanessa." When everybody was seated at the dinner table
Gwen's father said, "I heard alot of complaints from Gwen
is this true Vanessa?" "No they are not true" "Anthony how
could you talk to her like that." Gwendolynia is telling the
truth. "I'm going upstairs" said Van. "Why are you running
away are you afraid to hear the truth?" "Gwen stop that"
"Alice leave her alone ever since Vanessa came in here you
seem like you don't care for Gwen." "You better show a
little more likeness for Gwen or I'm going to court." "Alright

Tony, don't raise your voice." "Now you go to Gwen and
Van and you talk to them, Gwen is going to make eleven
tomorrow and you treat her like she was your baby. She's
growing up you have to treat her better now. Go and talk
to them I'm right behind you." Gwen's father and mother
came in the room then Gwen's mother said, "Vanessa you
shouldn't tell stories on Gwen its not nice." "I'm sorry, I
didn't mean to." "It's Gwen's birthday tomorrow, she's making eleven and I want you to be nice to her because she did
a lot for you, Gwen always wanted a sister and I got her
one, she is nice to you so will you please be nice to her."
"What time is it Alice?" "It's seven." "Where's Gwen?" "She
went to the store seven block away." "You should have sent
Van with her." "Here she comes now."

"Thanks Gwen, Start getting ready for bed so you can go
to church tomorrow." "Okay good night." The next morning
Gwen's parents were getting everything for the party, in the
afternoon Gwen and Vanessa went to church. They were just
coming home when Gwen said, "Mother Van behaved good at
Sunday School, she is in my class." "That's nice, did you
invite all your friends?" "Yes mom." Later in the afternoon,
about three, Van and Gwen were upstairs dressing for the
party then Gwen said, "Here is my best party dress, you
could have it if you want." "If you wanted my party dress
why didn't you say so, here you can have it." "I didn't want
your party dress, I asked if you wanted mine." "Well lets
go downstairs, my friends will be here any minute now."
"Gwen answer the door please." "Ok" "Hello Gwen and
Happy Birthday, here is a present for you." "Where is your
sister Beverly?" "She's coming."
     DING DONG
"Hello Karen." "Hello Gwen, here's a present." "Thank
you." DING DONG "Hello Marie, hi Dorothy, hi Barbie."
"Happy Birthday Gwen." "Happy Birthday Gwen." "Happy
Birthday Gwen." The door rang 14 more times, the last
time it was Beth Moon. At the party they played records
then everybody had a chance to talk. Then Beth Moon with
her fast mouth said, "How come you are wearing Gwendolyn's dress, don't you have any clothing of your own?"
"BETH" "When you came from the orphanage did you have
anything to wear?" "Beth Moon shut up." "I'm sorry." Then
Vanessa said to Gwen, "I bet you told all your friends about
my clothing and that I came from an orphanage." "Vanessa"
"Well I did come from an orphanage and as for you Gwendo-

lyn Green, I hate you." "Van where are you going?" "I wish
to go upstairs now." "It's all your fault Beth, you should
have kept your mouth shut."

"I'm sorry" said Beth. The party was over at 7:00 everybody went home, then Gwen's Mother said, "Gwen what
happened?" Beth Moon said "how come she is worrying my
dear that Vanessa went mad?" "You better go upstairs and
cheer her up" "okay Mom" "Van I am sorry for what happened." "That's okay I was silly to act up I should have
slapped her instead." "Vanessa I am sorry for what happened really I am I am getting ready for bed and do you
want to share my perfume?" "No no no I'll buy my own."
"Have it your own way, why are you acting so smart?"
"Mind your own business"

## III  JEALOUS

Five years passed and Vanessa and Gwen were 16 years
old. One day Gwen came home and said, "Mom I like a boy
in my class named Tom Johnson and he liked me until I
told Van." "Van I am glad you came down I have something
to tell you" "I heard what you told Mother but Tom Johnson
likes me we met yesterday. "That's not true because he's coming to take me to a movie later." "He's taking me to the
movie not you he doesn't like you just because you have
blue eyes, blonde hair, red lips you want all the boys in the
school to go after you" "Get out of my way Van I am getting dressed so when Tom comes he'll take me out. I found
someone to like me you got jealous and tried to take him
away from me, but little sister I am getting dressed so when
Tom comes he'll take me out." The doorbell rang and Gwen
went to answer it was Tom. Then Van called out "I'll be
right down Tom." "I thought you came for me" said Gwen.
"Good-bye Gwen dear" "Tomorrow I'll take you out Gwen,"
said Tom. "Never mind Tom Johnson." Then Van said before she walked out, "Don't mind her she's just Jealous."
"Mother did you see that? "That's what I had to go through
dear it'll work out somehow." "Not with Vanessa around."
"Gwen why don't you and I go to the beach tomorrow and
Van and Tom go out together." "okay that's a nice idea"
When Vanessa came home Gwen was sleeping, then Van
came in her Mother's room and said, "Mother Tom's taking
me to the beach tomorrow." "That's nice which beach? "The
one two blocks away from here, I wish it was farther." "That's

the one Gwen and I are going to." "That's nice" "Well I'm going to sleep." The next morning Tom came to pick up Vanessa later on Gwen and her Mother went. When Gwen got there she saw Tom and Van. Tom kept on looking straight at her. When Van went to the store, Tom came over to Gwen and said, How about a swim Gwen? "Do you think Van well be mad?" "No come on." "okay" Van came back and she saw Gwen and Tom in the water and she shouted at Tom "Come on out." "I'll be out in a second," said Tom. When Gwen came out of the water she went where her Mother was sitting. "Then she said they're going home." The next few days Van got sick. Tom was taking Gwen out. The first night when Gwen told Tom that Van was sick he said "Good" "I thought you liked her" "No she's too selfish" "Shh suppose she hears you." "I wish she did, I'm willing to take you out if you want." "Stay right here until I get my coat." "I bought a box of candy." "For me oh Thank-you." Tom and Gwen were in a restaurant then tom said, "I really don't like your sister I like you, Van said you treat her like a child. She thinks I go for her, but I don't sorry to say. "I like you too Tom." When they came home at 10:00, Van was in a chair downstairs. She said, "I heard what Tom said to you." "So sorry Van" "You're always sorry aren't you." "It wasn't my fault if he didn't like you Goodnight." "What has he done to me" "Don't cry Darling, You'll find someone else." One day Van and Gwen had an argument about Tom, Van said, "As soon as I was sick you stole him from me." "He didn't like you." "I don't believe you." "You don't have to, well Tom is mine, all mine and there is nothing you can do about it."

## IV   DON'T TREAT ME LIKE A CHILD

"I'll find another boy for you." "GWEN WOULD YOU STOP TREATING ME LIKE A CHILD." "Am sorry Van." "Sorry, sorry, sorry, am tired of your soriness." "Goodnight, Van." "Van, Van, Van, she even has the manner to say goodnight." Van got up the next morning and found her breakfast on the table, she threw it on the floor and said, "Am not a child any more I could fix my own breakfast." Then mother came out and said, "What's the meaning of throwing this breakfast on the floor." "Gwen made it." "Correction I made it." "Well you can't blame me." "Gwen get the stick." "Here it is."
WAP, WAP, WAP

"oops, ouch." "Now don't come down until I call you."
When Gwen went upstairs to Van, Van said, "I'm sorry for
all the trouble I caused you, I really am." "This is the first
time in your life you sound real sorry, it don't seem like we're
sisters, it seems like we're strangers." "Am running away."
"You can't do that." "Oh yes I can."

"You're going to sit down like a good girl, remember
am older than you." "Gwen stop treating me like a child for
heavens sake." "Vanessa Green I were doing everything for
you since you moved in this house. If it wasn't for me, you
would have still be in the orphanage or working, you have to
respect me and everybody else around you, remember that."

SLAM Gwen ran out in the garden and bumped into
father, he said, "Hi, pet where's Van." "Mother has her
punished." "Why, what she done." "Mother fixed her some
breakfast, since she got up late. Then she took all the food
that mother fixed and threw it on the floor." "What" "Then
she had the nerve to say that she thought I fixed it." "Oh I
get it, she deserves a punishment for a change." "She told
me she was running away, if it wasn't for me she would have
been working now." "I want to have a talk with her." "She's
upstairs." While Gwen's father was speaking to Van, Gwen
went to help her mother in the kitchen. Gwen said, "Dad's
upstairs talking to Van." "Van says she is running away."
"She'll need money." "Oh you know Van, she'll steal it." "If
she ran away and stole money, they'll put her in a home for
girls." "If she were 18, she'll go to prison." "Here comes
your father, and he has a smile on his face." "Dad, why are
you smiling, did Van sweet-talk you." "She said, she had a
sterling headache, and she send her to bed like that." "Gwen
get me the stick, if she is going to start telling lies on me I
have to straighten her up", said Mother. Mother went upstairs and whipped Van 16 times right on her butt, and then
mother put down the stick and said, "you're a great liar."
Mother gave Van 16 slaps on her mouth and said, "see if
you can use your mouth now. Make one more trouble and
I'm putting you away in a girls home, remember that." As
soon as Van's mother left the room, Van started to pack. As
soon as everybody went to sleep, Van stole some of Gwen's
money, and crept out the window.

When she was outside she went to get a bus. She didn't
know where to go. The next morning she found herself besides the Atlantic Ocean. When Gwen woke up and found
out Vanessa was gone she looked in the drawer, Van's

clothing was gone. Her money was gone too, she shouted,
"Mom, Dad, come quick." "What's wrong pet?"' "Van's
gone." "Alice come quick, Vanessa is gone. Call the police,
she took Gwen's money." The next day they found Van. She
was in a terrible condition. She was in the hospital for a
week. When she came out she was a nice girl, she treated
Gwen and her parents nice. This went on for a long time
until Gwen and Vanessa married. They had a nice family
and they lived happily every after.

**THE END**

IT WAS IN APRIL, after their move to the new school, that I talked to the class about my limitations within the educational system. Before that, however, I found myself telling them about the demands that the system made upon them. There were compulsory achievement and, at that time, IQ, tests given halfway through the year, and it was on the results of those tests that the children's placement in junior high school would be based. Nothing else really counted; classes were formed on the basis of reading grades and my pupils *had* to do well. It was a matter of their whole future since in junior high school all but those few students put in the "top" classes (three out of fourteen on each grade) were considered "not college material" and treated with the scorn that they merited in their teachers' eyes.

The easiest way to bring this up in class was to tell the children exactly where they stood. I braced myself, and defying all precedent as well as my own misgivings, I performed the unforgivable act of showing the children what their reading and IQ scores were according to the record cards. I also taught a lesson on the definition of IQ and of achievement scores. The children were angry and shocked; no one had ever come right out and told them they were failing. It was always put so nicely and evasively that the children never knew where they stood. After seeing the IQ scores—only two of which were above 100, the majority being in the 80 to 90 range—and the reading scores, which with few exceptions were below grade level, the children were furious. I asked them what they wanted to do about it, and sadly they threw back at me:

"Mr. Kohl, what can we do about it?"

And I told them. Only I didn't say read more, or take remedial lessons, or spend another year in school, and you will be better off. I told them what middle-class teachers usually tell their pupils, what I heard myself while in public school in New York City, and what teachers in Harlem are usually too honest and scrupulous to tell their pupils. I said if you listen I will teach you how to take tests and how to get around them.

This scrupulosity of Harlem teachers and administrators with respect to tests is a curious psychological phenomenon, completely at variance with the irresponsibility they display in all other educational and disciplinary matters. Yet I think it is all too easily explicable. They feel their own failures with the children are vindicated if an objective test, objectively administered, shows the child to be a failure.

There were no sample tests available, to prepare the children beforehand. The assistant principal told me that if old tests were made available the children would have an unfair advantage over other children. I reminded him that keeping files of old tests was frequently standard procedure at middle-class schools, and that P.S. 6, a predominantly white school located less than a mile down Madison Avenue even gave after-school voluntary classes in test preparation. He shrugged and told me that a rule was a rule. So I went to friends who taught in white schools and got copies of the old tests and sample questions that they used and went ahead with my plans. No one checked on what I was doing, and no one really cared as long as my class wasn't disruptive.

The first thing I had to do was familiarize the children with test instructions. I spent several weeks on practicing following directions as they are worded on the standard tests. The class asked me why such practice was necessary, and I explained that with all the fine writing they could produce, with all the words of praise and recommendation I could write, they would go nowhere in junior high school unless those grades on paper were up to the standards the Board of Education set. The kids didn't like that idea, I don't like it; but we had to get tough and face the fact that like it or not they *had* to do well. When I put it that way they were willing to try.

After going through the reading of directions, I broke down the types of questions that were asked on the various reading tests and tried to explain something of the psychology of the people who created the test. I frequently found that some of the children were deliberately choosing wrong answers because they had clever explanations for their choices. They had to be convinced that the people who created objective tests believed as an article of faith that all the questions they made up had one and only one correct answer. Over and over, it is striking how rigid teachers tend to be and how difficult it is for children who haven't been clued in on this rigidity to figure out what the teacher expects in the way of suppression of original and clever responses. The children agreed to be dull for the sake of their future.

After these exercises we simulated testing situations, and the children gradually learned to cease dreading and avoid-

ing the testing situation. Their anxiety decreased to a man-
ageable level, and therefore they were able to apply things
they had discovered in their own thinking, reading, and
writing to situations that arose in the test.

Unfortunately I had no say in determining when the
tests were given. Both the reading and IQ tests had to be
given before February for administrative reasons, and so the
full benefit of the year's work did not show in those tests.
The IQ test was close to a disaster. True, there were about
ten children who came up over 100 and one—Grace—who
scored 135, but the children were not yet able to cope with
the test and didn't show themselves as well as they could.
With the reading test it was different. The children were
almost ready and in a few short months performed the
seemingly impossible task of jumping from one to three
years in reading. There were a few children on fifth-grade
level, about twelve on sixth-grade level, another twelve on
seventh-grade level, and eight who ranged from the eighth to
the twelfth grades. I couldn't believe it myself. When I told
the results to the children, they for once showed their pride
in themselves unashamedly.

The children learned that they could do unpleasant but
necessary work; they also knew that the test preparation was
not all there was to education, that the substance of their
work, the novels and stories, the poems and projects they created, were the essential thing no matter how the external
world chose to judge them. They were proud of their work
and themselves. I felt thrilled and privileged to teach them
and witness them create. I offered what I could to them;
they offered much in return. I am grateful that over the course
of the year I could cease to be afraid and therefore respond
to what the children had to teach me of myself, of themselves
and the world they lived in and which we shared as human
beings.

Not all of the children made it through the year; two
moved, and one, John, was too much for me to control. He
was tough and shook my confidence. It would take me another year before I could reach children like him. We never
fought, he didn't disrupt the class; he just disappeared into
the halls and then the streets. I have to admit that I made
a very feeble and false effort to stop him; the rest of the
class occupied me. The next year I had a class of Johns, and
seeing how easily they responded to adult confidence and
trust, I have always regretted my lack of effort with John.
Yet I have to admit that I did not have the necessary confidence as a teacher and as a human being the year I taught

the thirty-six children. It took the thirty-six children to give me that.

The year did not come to a conclusion. It ended as all school years must. Michael was beginning his third novel, Sam was starting his first. It was the end of June; commencement came with its absurd pomp, and then a farewell party. The children had to move across the street to junior high school and to a new, more chaotic and difficult world.

# PART TWO

# *A Dream Deferred*

What happens to a dream deferred?

Does it dry up
like a raisin in the sun?
Or fester like a sore—
And then run?
Does it stink like rotten meat?
Or crust and sugar over—
like a syrupy sweet?

Maybe it just sags
like a heavy load.

*Or does it explode?*

LANGSTON HUGHES
*Harlem*

THE FOLLOWING SEPTEMBER meant meeting new children, concentrating my energy and feelings on them and letting go of my preoccupation with the thirty-six children. It was sad yet exciting, beginning again with an empty classroom. I waited nervously for the children, refusing to think of my first words. At nine o'clock they came in quietly and hesitantly, looking me over. They were nervous too. I looked at my new class and told them how strange it felt to be in school again, starting another year, meeting new people. They agreed. One boy said he almost stayed home. A girl, Alice, said she came because she knew that she'd be having a man teacher. At that I introduced myself and asked the class to sit in any seats they liked. Everyone looked at me, puzzled. Then a big boy, Willie, said:

"You mean I don't have to sit in the back?"

"No."

"And you're not going to keep me at your desk to watch me?"

"Why, should I watch you?"

"Didn't they tell you?"

"Nobody told me anything about the class, I didn't ask. This is a new year, everyone starts from the beginning."

Our first day of school was not like my first day with 6-1. I felt free to encounter the children without preconceptions and explore with them what was meaningful to learn. The children didn't frighten me; there was no question of control since I knew I was in control of myself. Time and chaos weren't my enemies—a bit of disorder, time to explore and play were all expected to be part of our year together. I had no trouble talking to the class. In a sense we started together and therefore could plunge into things more quickly than was possible with 6-1.

Other teachers had warned me of my new class—it was 6-7, "the bottom." I was told that the children were illiterate, indifferent, dangerous. Someone claimed that most of them wouldn't even show up after the first week. In June some colleagues, as the children suspected, offered to point out "the ones" who would cause me the most trouble. I declined just as I had declined to look at the children's record cards in September.

The children looked older than the ones in 6-1, taller and more self-assured. They spoke about themselves freely and with great perception. They knew that they were rejects in the school, and they also knew that the school as a whole was a reject. Any adult pretense of the opposite would have closed them up altogether.

As soon as everyone was settled I began as directly as possible and asked the class what books they wanted to read. Naturally they asked for sixth grade readers. I told them I felt the books were too hard and they groaned.

"We're not so dumb, Mr. Kohl."

"I won't do that baby stuff again."

"Mr. Kohl, we can read anything."

I asked the children how well they thought they read and they became confused; no one had ever told them. They only knew that every year they got the same second- and third-grade books, which they knew by heart. My first lesson became clear. I took out the class record cards and dumped them on my desk. Then I explained to the class what grade reading scores meant, and what the significance of IQ was.

"If you are reading up to your grade level, that means in the sixth grade, you're supposed to have a score in the sixes; six point zero, six point one, and so forth. If you have average intelligence your IQ should be at least one hundred. Let's see what these cards say."

There was suspense in the room as I listed the scores: 3.1, 3.4, 2.0, 4.2, 3.1 . . . IQ's of 70, 75, 81, 78 . . . then anger.

"Mr. Kohl we're not that dumb."

"It's phoney."

"No one taught us that stuff, no one ever told us."

But they knew now. After a heated debate I threw my first question back at the class.

"Tell me what books you want to read."

The class chose fifth-grade books, ones they knew would be difficult for them in preference to ones that were on their supposed "level." They were ready to fight to read and learn, met my challenge, and kept on challenging themselves and me for the rest of the year.

One day during the first week Alice coyly proposed a bet.

"Mr. Kohl, I bet I can read anything on your desk no matter what those cards of yours say."

Her reading score was 3.4. I accepted and she went through all the books on my desk including a page of the novel I was reading on the way to school. I was perplexed and delighted.

"How can you do that and still have a three point four reading score?"

"I wouldn't read for those teachers. Listen——"

Alice picked up a book and stumbled through several paragraphs. She paused, stuttered, committed omissions and reversals, *i.e.*, read on a low third-grade level. Then she looked at my astonished face and burst out laughing.

Alice was tough and angry and brilliant. She was hypersensitive and incapable of tolerating insult or prejudice. In her previous years in school she had been alternately defiant and withdrawn. She was considered a "troublemaker" by some teachers, "disturbed" by others. Yet when offered something substantial, a serious novel, for example, or the opportunity to write honestly, she blossomed. During the year she became hungry to learn and less hostile. It was sometimes hard to find material to keep up with her voracious appetite.

Juan sat next to Alice in the front of the room, quiet and quixotic. When there was a good deed to be done Juan would be certain to volunteer and mess things up. He was shy, and according to the records I showed him had an IQ of 70 and was illiterate.

He listened intensely in class when I taught reading; otherwise he seemed to be somewhere else. He never spoke in class; yet after the Christmas holiday he came to me and told me that I had taught him how to read. It seemed that the idea that words were divided into syllables excited him, and so over the Christmas vacation he divided all the names under *A* in the phone book into syllables and learned how to read. I was astonished at his excitement over a fact of grammar that seemed dull and matter-of-fact to me. I encouraged Juan to write, and for all his struggle with the English language a beautiful, sad world emerged.

One cold rainy day I was going to school and I had to go 1,000 miles to get there and there wasn't no cars and no buses and train so I had to walk. I got soke a wet. I still had 500 more miles to go at last I almost got there and went I got there the school was close and I thought for a minute and then I remember it was a haliday and then I droped deid.

It rains too much and my flowers vegetable and gardens they get too much water. I got to think of something fast because if it keeps on like this my plants can't grow. So one day I was walking in the street when I saw this store selling rain supplies so I went in and got some then I went back

home and I had one that will just rite rain so I planted in the
ground and the next day I couldn't believe my eyes all the
plants were just growing up. So I live happily ever after.

I just don't like to think because every time I think I
get a headache because one time I was thinking about the
world fair and I build a mental picture in my mind I was
enjoying myself then I stop thinking. I was going home went
suddenly I felt something in my mind and I got a headache
and I was criing because my mind hurt. From that day on
I can't think.

It happens every time I go to bed I forget to brush your
teeth. Then the second time I forget to brush your teeth.
Then the second time I forgot the third time I forgot too
so I had to do something, so one day I was very sleepy I
was going to my bed then sudently I open my eyes then I
remember and I ran back to bath tob and I brush my teeth
you didn't got me this time so I went back to bed and then
every single day I brush my teeth live happily ever after.

Not all the children were as talented or imaginative as
Juan and Alice, just as not everyone was as inspired as
Robert or Alvin in 6-1. Yet many things developed in the
classroom; much passed between the children and myself. I
was a much better listener than I had been the previous
year, and consequently it seemed to me that the children
talked more—of their families and friends, of life on the
streets and its seductive ways. The boys spoke at length and
in detail; individual conversations grew into group discussions
and debates. I began to offer some relevant psychology and
history and so together we redesigned the curriculum once
more—but, that's another book. It is sufficient here to say
that the children were alive and real for me—during the
middle of the year it seemed as if 6-7 were the only class I
had ever taught or wanted to teach. The year had a logic
of its own as does every school year, every class of children.
Once teachers can forget how a class should be they can
discover each year what it must be like with that specific
class at that particular moment in their lives.

I noticed many things during that school year that I had
previously protected myself from. The insecurity of working
in a new school with unknown children had passed. I no
longer had to struggle with my fear and insecurity or worry
about maintaining order and filling up time. I had faith in

my work and the children and with that perspective it was no longer necessary to shut out the rest of the school.

I guess even if I had wanted to, the children in 6-7 wouldn't have let me. They knew they were the school's rejects and were treated with less warmth and respect than any other pupils. They knew how they were being abused, and once they found an adult they could trust and talk to they insisted upon documenting the horrors of that indifferent institution. That is one of the problems of speaking freely and honestly—the truth can become a dangerous burden.

The children described the teachers in the school, the books and supplies, the administration, other children, themselves . . . I listened carefully and made the time to verify their perceptions. At times I contradicted the children, made my experience and perception relevant. Yet for the most part the children were right, and I had to allow into my consciousness things it had been easier to ignore or suppress.

I attended to teachers' conversations, listened to them abuse the children until I could no longer go into the teachers' lunchroom. The most frequent epithet they used in describing the children was "animals." After a while the word "animal" came to epitomize for me most teachers' ambiguous relations to ghetto children—the scorn and the fear, the condescension yet the acknowledgment of some imagined power and unpredictability. I recognized some of that in myself, but never reached the sad point of denying my fear and uncertainty by projecting fearsome and unpredictable characteristics on the children and using them in class as some last primitive weapon. It was pitiful yet disgusting, all the talk of "them," "these children," "animals." I remember a teacher from another school I taught in, a white Southerner with good intentions and subtle and unacknowledged prejudices. He fought for the good part of a semester to gain the children's attention and affection. He wanted the children to listen to him, to respond to him, to learn from him; yet never thought to listen, respond, or learn from the children, who remained unresponsive, even sullen. They refused to learn, laughed at his professed good intentions, and tested him beyond his endurance. One day in rage and vexation it all came out.

"Animals, that's what you are, animals, wild animals, that's all you are or can be."

His pupils were relieved to hear it at last, their suspicions were confirmed. They rose in calm unison and slowly circled the raging trapped teacher, chanting, "We are animals, we are animals, we are animals . . . ," until the bell rang and mercifully broke the spell. The children ran off, leaving the broken, confused man wondering what he'd done, convinced that he had always been of goodwill but that "they" just couldn't be reached.

It wasn't only the teachers, and it wasn't all of them either. There were a few who knew and loved the children, who stayed in the school heartbroken, year after year, watching the other teachers, being abused by the administration, seeing the children fail and nobody care. I became friendly with one such teacher—he had been at the school for twelve years and all of the children there knew him. He knew them too, and was constantly besieged by visitors, kids passed out of the school system returning to talk and feel that some element in the world was constant and available.

I could see how much the children needed him, and he loved them. Yet the contrast between this concern and his barren classroom upset me. The bulletin boards were bare, the cabinets empty. There was no sign of children's work or activity. The room was hardly inhabited. He seldom taught anything or bothered with the few books that were available, and seemed content to let his pupils talk and relax. I could see throwing out the nonsense, but resting there, with nothing else to offer, seemed worse than resigning oneself to the standard curriculum. It took me several weeks to gather courage to confront him with my puzzlement—how could he stand not offering something to the children, not finding a way to teach, since he so obviously cared. He looked deeply hurt at my remarks, almost walked away, but answered.

"One good year is not enough to help the children make it out of this jungle. The next year whatever they learned will be unlearned, their confidence and pride swept away, destroyed. It's good for them to know at one point in their lives that someone, even a teacher, cares, that they can do anything anyone else can. But that's immediately undermined by the hundreds of teachers who don't care. For eight years I sweated, spent my life for the kids, following as many as I could into junior high school, high school, trying at the same time to give something to my sixth-graders. I was an unwilling Penelope, seeing the work I had done come undone before my eyes, seeing children who had left my class with hope return beat and confused. The reason so many kids come back to visit is not because of what I taught— they forget that—but because at one time they were safe here, protected from the indifference and cruelty of the system. They can talk to me of their failure and despair—unfortunately I understand it. Four years ago I got tired of seeing my work undone. I can't do it anymore, so I go through the motions and let the kids relax. I should quit and fight the whole thing somehow but I'm too weak . . . been a teacher too long, I need that security, the vacations. . . ."

His voice trailed off as I retreated to my classroom thinking, *it can't happen to 6-1,* not quite daring to look at my present work in the fearful perspective of the future, almost hoping not to see the children again so I would not know how hard a time they were having and how little my work had come to. But I had to look; it was forced on me in late November when the thirty-six children began to visit and hint to me of their failure and despair.

Alvin and Robert Jackson were the first visitors. They waited after school one Friday. We greeted joyously, gossiped about the class and the summer. I introduced them to Alice who always hung round until I left and then asked about school. Robert looked toward Alvin, who blushed, then shrugged his shoulders. Robert pushed him.

"You tell him, Chipmunk."

"Mr. Kohl, this English teacher, she's dumb. I mean she won't answer any questions like you did. She took Robert's book away because we're not allowed to write in class. She threw it in the basket without even looking at it."

"What'd you do?"

"Tell him, Robert."

"I walked out, but I got the book first. I knew there was going to be trouble when she told us to write about ourselves the first day. She wrote across my paper, Too much violence and fighting, and failed me."

It wasn't only English that was giving them trouble. In math the teacher refused to answer questions; in social studies they were learning about the blessings of American democracy once more. They had a good science teacher though. Small comfort. Already in November, Robert and Alvin were once more resigned to the fact that school was an unpleasant experience at best.

I was shaken by our meeting and spent that weekend thinking out my work. I remembered one day, just before graduation. Robert and Alvin were with me. It was three o'clock and they walked me into the principal's office where I had to sign out.

The principal, an amiable man, approached the boys and asked how they were doing. They shrugged, but I insisted they tell about their writing and art. Robert wouldn't, so I talked glowingly of his work.

"Really? Well Robert, I'd like to see your work."

The principal produced a flower pot with a plant in it, a pencil, and paper. Robert studied the plant for a moment, then produced an extraordinarily detailed and accurate drawing.

The principal was impressed, muttered some words of praise, then took the pencil from Robert and signed the drawing himself. Then he gave it to Robert as a souvenir.

Gave it to Robert!

I couldn't forget that incident all summer and now with Robert's book going into the wastebasket and Alvin's remaining home unfinished, unread, the scorn and lack of respect adults feel toward the children and their work hurt and confused me. Why cause more trouble for the children by teaching well, allowing them to write and question, to live honestly in the classroom? It only invites trouble and failure in school. Perhaps it would have been better to have kept the standard curriculum and develop a "professional" attitude and not disrupt the children's lives—for that is what happened that last year in school. It wasn't only or even the writing and art the children created that was most important. Rather it was that over a year together the children came to expect things of themselves and from the classroom that they had not conceived of before. But I did not foresee the subsequent disappointment of the children's expectations in other classrooms, and the bitterness it would create. Better perhaps not to create hope, to fail like most other teachers and pretend it was the children's fault. I was confused and angry at myself, more so that Monday I had to return to school and my present class—twenty-four more children who were beginning to think differently of themselves and school. It had been a long uncomfortable weekend.

I returned to school Monday and immediately got caught up in my work, unable and unwilling to think the dilemma through to a conclusion.

I also tried to provide Robert and Alvin with some partial substitute for school—music and art lessons. Alvin quickly lost interest but Robert continued throughout the year.

Robert and Alvin weren't the only ones having trouble in school; Ralph, Maurice, Charles, Michael—they all came back discouraged and demoralized. It was the same with the girls. Margie stopped going to school altogether, while Carol, Barbara, Dianne, most of the others, dragged their bodies in to school, occasionally listened, were sometimes defiant, but for the most part sat listlessly through the meaningless day.

Some of the children were luckier. Grace was in a special class for gifted children which meant that she went out of the district because only one of the junior high schools in Harlem had classes for the gifted. Pamela, Gail, Neomia, and Leverne managed to get into integrated middle-class junior highs, and though the adjustment was difficult, found the challenge of actually competing with white children stimulating. Desiree and Thomas C., on the other hand, found the pressure too great, the whites too hostile, and wanted to return to ghetto schools.

I watched the children's struggles, tried to help and at the same time prepare another group of children to go on in school and the world. I observed the school around me, and the number of children not even receiving the little I had to offer. I felt isolated and angry, yet refused to give up on either the children in 6-1 or those in 6-7. If the children failed it was my failure as a teacher for not teaching well enough or not knowing the right things to teach. I refused to fall into the trap many ghetto teachers make for themselves: if a child fails it's his fault; no need to adjust what's taught; just blame the environment, the family, the administration. Such rigidity only increases the children's failures and the teacher's convictions of the child's inability to succeed, leads to frustration and ultimately to covert prejudice and hostility. Yet how to discover what is right to teach, how to fight in a single classroom the monumental indifference of an entire system, how to help the thirty-six children now grown to sixty? I struggled with those questions, talked to the children of success and failure, of their strength and ability to overcome indifference and hostility. Words are so little, so temporary a solace.

I couldn't help Alvin from being torn apart by continually and subtly being treated as inferior by his English teacher, nor could I prevent Robert Jackson from exploding in class when an exasperated teacher called him stupid. At most I could be there for the children, a constant figure to listen and repeat that people are not lost because they may seem so and that life is not at an end because everything may seem at a given moment to be hopeless. The children understood this, went back into hated classrooms, fought, left, yet returned once more. There was something tenacious and tough about their determination to finish school.

I recently thought of this when I was working with some people in a high school in Harlem. Many of the teachers laughed at the children, believed they didn't care about school, or anything, for that matter. Yet these teachers couldn't see the sad fact that no matter how poorly their students, most of whom were over sixteen, the dropout age, did in school, still they came—with what magical hope that things would improve, that one day they would find themselves reading, graduating, in college . . . still they came and were laughed at for it. The guidance counselors, blind to the beauty and pathos of youngsters of eighteen and nineteen still trying where they have failed so often, usually recommended leaving school.

During that year with 6-7 doubts began to possess me and steal the joy of seeing the children working and learning. I was no longer sure of the value of my work to the children. That it helped me was undeniable. I arrived to teach 6-1, knowing little of the world and less of myself. I had a contract to write a book on contemporary philosophy, but confronted with the actual writing I froze. For a year I couldn't put down a word—I was too frightened of what other people would think, too worried about critics and success, to say what I felt honestly and directly. In December with 6-1, I experienced the irony of witnessing my pupils take out their books and write at nine in the morning while I stared at a blank piece of paper at nine at night. By April the paper was no longer blank, and by the end of the summer of 1963 my book, *The Age of Complexity,* was finished. I had watched the children writing, read their work, and understood what petty fear prevented me from saying what I felt and thought.

But that wasn't all. Confronted by the human challenge of the classroom I reached into myself, uncovered a constant core which enabled me to live with my mistakes and hypocrisies, my weaknesses and pettiness; to accept as myself all the many contrary and contradictory things I was. I fought to be more human and feel I succeeded. And because of all this I had to ask: What about the children? Of what worth is all this to the children? At one time I thought I knew, but not any longer. Certain uncomfortable questions became more and more insistent: Was it possible to function usefully within the existing school system? Must one get out and agitate to change the system? Or can one stay enclosed in a "successful" classroom ignoring everything that happens subsequently to one's pupils? By June of the year with 6-7, I was tired and lacked perspective. The thought of twenty-five more children the next year, twenty-five that might have a good year yet ultimately benefit little or nothing from it, depressed me. I wanted to think and to write, to discover how I could best serve the children.

*The Age of Complexity* was finished; there was an advance on the book, my summer pay. I decided to take a year's leave and go to Europe. As hard as it was to part

from the children, it was necessary, and so I spent a year in
Spain, thinking, mostly, and writing, avoiding until the last
moments the decision to return to work with the children
and still remain outside of the system. I have never stopped
teaching, but I no longer have a classroom. I meet with the
children—children no longer but young men and women—
have met their friends, and we steal a room wherever we
can: my home, Teachers College, Columbia, on Saturday
afternoon, a friend's office. We talk about things that are
relevant to life. Recently the kids have requested a series of
courses which fully shows where they are and what they want
to know.

Hostility and Aggression
How People Change and Are Changed
Evolution or Revolution
The Varieties of Love
Suicide and War
On Cooling Out
Control and Loss of Control
On Good and Evil
Can One Really Know Other People?
Fear and Loneliness
The Economics of Ambition and Goodness
The Self
Growth
The Place of Religion in Life
The Good Mother and the Bad Mother

There seems to be no end to the children's troubles, yet
there is no death of their joy. Robert Jackson, the author of
*A Barbarian Becomes a Greek Warrior* and *Journey Through
Time and Space,* the cartoonist, mythologist, and artist, after
a difficult year in one junior high school was transferred to
another and "rediscovered." Somehow he managed to find a
teacher who listened when Robert claimed he could draw and
write. His work impressed the teacher, and so Robert became one of the twenty or so students in his junior high
school who, according to the staff, could be "saved." Giving up
on 90 percent of the students, the teachers lavished attention
upon Robert and the few others whose talents were suffi-
ciently developed so that a little encouragement would almost
guarantee success. The staff developed a stake in Robert; he
was a verification that they weren't totally indifferent or in-
competent. Every positive gesture he made was reinforced,
sometimes to the detriment of his self-respect. A lazy draw-

ing or indifferent story was praised lavishly because his teachers feared that without praise he would fail. The opposite
may have been true: Robert might have done better and
respected his work more if it had been treated with greater
honesty and integrity. However, his junior high school teachers succeeded in the sense that they wanted to succeed. After
two years in junior high Robert was admitted to Music and
Art High School on the basis of recommendations and an
entrance examination. He may have been the first graduate
of my school to pass the exam.

When I was in Spain Robert and I corresponded. He
told me of his life, his awakening consciousness of society and
art, of joy and a hard-won, tenuous optimism. I ignored the
undercurrents, Robert's inability to pay for postage, the boy-
cotts, Malcolm. . . .

October 17, 1964

Dear Mr. and Mrs. Kohl,

I am still on that last book that you saw, which is en-
titled, "Best Stories of R.G.J.". It is about a negro boy who
is eighteen, and sits in the penetentary waiting for his older
criminal brother to rescue him. Finally, he finds out that his
brother still hasn't come, and a year later he is pardoned. So
right now he is searching for his brother, to team up with
him in the state of Georgia.

I have received all three of your letters, and have been
trying hard to answer them. Unfortunately, I have been having a hard time getting stamps.

Alvin is not going to my junior high school this fall.
His mother has decided to transfer him to a school in Brook-
lyn. I hear his doing fine, and that he will come back to
Manhattan to visit.

The battle for the Presidency and Senate is on. Johnson
and Humphrey were chosen for the democratic nominees,
Goldwater and Miller for the Republican parties. It seems
most likely that the Johnson-Humphrey team will dominate
the office because, in my neighborhood, the negroes, (I think
all who vote) are voting democratic. For the senate, there's
Robert Kennedy on the democratic party, and Kenneth
Keating, the republican. I don't know who will win between
these two because: Robert Kennedy is supported by negroes
because he is the brother of the dead president. Kenneth
Keating is supported by negroes because they say he helped

the negroes down in Birmingham. Frankly, I don't care who
becomes president or senetor, I'm just R.G.J!

You know, I went to Alabama not so long ago (it was
my first time in the south). I hated the smell, looks, and
even some of the people there! . . . Those crazy accents,.
and crazy way of doing things! The white people down there
stares at you as if you or they were crazy!

And so much for that. As for Music and Art High
School, I can't qualify until the ninth grade. The only tests
available are Brooklyn Tech, and Bronx Science. If I wait
for Music and Art in the ninth grade, it may be too late! I
want to hurry up and get out of junior high school right
away!

Mr. Kohl, could you please tell me (if you know how to
read, play, or write music) a little understanding of music?

I know how to read, and play music, but the writing
part I don't get. So could you please, if you can, help me in
writing music?

Do you know that the girls in our class are very pretty?
Man! They have nice shapes, nice looks, and everything!
Incidently, you remember Barbara ——. She's in my class
from the Annex this year.

I hope I told you all that could interest you. I've tried
to write all I can, and I guess it's time for me to go now.
The family is doing fine . . . and life is running much more
harder, since I'm older.

Yours truely,
R. G. Jackson

Novembre 25, 1964

Dear Mr. and Mrs. Kohl,

I have recieved your seven-page letter and the music
paper. I have also recieved the stamps, and I am very grateful for them.

I would like to inform you on a few things: first, I
think I am happier now because of this, and I think you
should be also. I have gotten transfered from Junior High
School ——, and into J.H.S. ——. This term, the ——
Junior High has sixth, seventh, and eigth grades, so now I
can graduate in the eigth grade, and go to Music and Art!
They also gave me my application, a few days ago for

Music and Art and some of the qualifications in the portfolio I must have work done in pen and ink, charcoal, and pastels, paint, pencil, stillife, landscapes, portraits, scenery, etc. In the music department, you must either sing or play an instrument, but if I get there, I will try for composition, and probably band arrangements in music.

Incidentally, the reason I was transferred from Junior High School ——, was because I was out of their district, and since the school was getting crowded, I was moved.

The systems in —— are far more different than that of ——, 'cause if you do anything wrong, like sassy back at the teacher, or fool around, he takes out a paddle and he bends you over a chair so that your tail is sticking up and WHAMO! That's why I don't joke around. And in gym, if you are late for exercizes, or are unprepared, you get the same treatment. They say that —— is worse than ——, it's not true, not if you stay there for about a year. In ——, the teachers don't care if you don't want to learn or not, they just give you a zero and let you have your way, but in ——, your back part will be burning if you refuse to do any work, or don't pay attention. The teachers there make you learn, and they speak to you in profane language, and in the same way your parents do. (It's an all boys school also).

Mr. Kohl, if you are writing to Alvin, would you please tell me what and how he is doing, and give me his address so that I can write to him also? I would appreciate it very much.

I have found a new method of composing tunes, and have come up with about ten. It's sure good to have an organ around! Later on, I will send you some of the songs that Lawrence Smith and I have composed.

Sincerely yours,
*Robert George Jackson*

February 4, 1965

Dear Mr. and Mrs. Kohl,

My Christmas vacation was fine, and I recieved your present just in time for Christmas. I think you will have tell me how to open, load and close the pen, because I can't read the Spanish instructions that came with it.

I have already taken the exam for Music and Art in the middle of January. The test was very easy, and I'm sure I'm going to pass it. We had to draw from Observation, Memory, and Imagination. I will be getting the results of the test in April.

I have recieved your book and it looks like a hard book to read. I like the cover arrangement and the title. It sure must be strange to see your name written all over the book like that.

There was another Boycott in our neighborhood which started on January 22. . . . The main thing they did this for was for FREEDOM!

I haven't written any stories too much, except one for my teacher who is placing it in our school magazine along with my pictures. I have been writting poems and lyrics for music though. I've also written and composed a lot of music of my own . . .

I've been thinking of a lot about music, and every piece of music I hear, I listen to it closely and see how it is composed. Classical, Contemporary, and Jazz. There's a group called the "Kinks" (only stupid names like that comes from England) and their songs are very, very simple. If you listen to their music, you can tell how it is composed. I also try to listen to the radio a lot to hear how these groups sound, play, etc. I'm very much interested in recording on a real record label, and I wonder if you could tell me how the regular contemporary group starts out in doing so, the people he works for, the money, etc. Alvin keeps insisting on being a saxiphonist instead of a drummer. My mom always scolded me for drumming on things, and I've found that I have a very good sense of rhythm. My voice is very deep, and it doesn't sound too well for singing, so I might just be our drummer, leader, and song writer.

I am sorry for not writing, but I have been studying for that music and art test, and getting my portfolio ready. I'm still going to try to send you a piece of my music, and soon as it's organized.

So, I would like to hear from you again, Mr. Kohl, and I will try to write as much as I can.

Yours Truely,
*R. G. Jackson*

March 10, 1965

Dear Mr. and Mrs. Kohl,

I must thank you for your information about music, and musicians, and the pen works beautifully (as you can see). I tried to write with it with black india ink, but it won't work too well because the ink dries out too fast. So I've tried some of these colored inks that you gave me, and they work fine.

As for music, I've never heard of Baby Dodds, but I'll look out for some of his recordings. I wonder if he hits the drums as much as Art Blakely (that's the real drummer), or Max Roach (he plays them as if he had roaches crawling all around the drums)? Neither have I heard of John Coltrane, and Charlie Mingus. Thelonious Monk is not so hot.

Let me tell you what's been going on in the boring American world: Malcolm X was shot to death last month on a Sunday. He was making a conference at the Audobon (where I had seen him before), when just before he was making his speech, a swarm of bullets hit him. A week before that, incidently, his house was burned down. Since he was kicked out of the Muslim organization, he blamed the Muslims for his house's damage. And, many people blamed the Muslims for his death, so they burned down the Muslim's Mosque on 116th street and Lenox Ave.

(Ah, hem!) My name was in the last week's Amsterdam News on one of the lists as outstanding in conduct. I sure wish I could send you a copy of that article, but I didn't find out about it until today!

You want to know something that would dissappoint you, Mr. Kohl? (HEH, HEH! I knew you would!) Your favorite girl pupil, Barbara is slipping in her conduct marks. Wanna know how I found out? My friend, Lawrence Smith tells me everything about ——. He said she chews gum in class, talks, laughs, etc. I know you can't believe it . . . but . . . I can't either!

As for the chipmunk, Alvin, he's probably hibernating over the winter. You'll hear from him next spring. But, seriously, I haven't seen or heard from Alvin ever since January. I'm making arrangements to see him next week.

Mr. Kohl, as a bonus for you, I'm going to send you a copy of our very first hit song: "HANG AROUND." The title's kinda funny, but you know how it is. It is written by

Lawrence Smith and me, and I would like to see how you and Judy approve of it. And so, for now, I will let the stamp and envelope do the rest, by transporting this letter to you.

*R. G. Jackson*

March 19, 1965

Dear Mr. and Mrs. Kohl,

I am very sorry for this typewritten letter. The reason for it is because I had sent out a letter a day after you had sent your last letter, and I stuck some thick paper inside. I folded it up too thick. Thus, the post office sent it back saying I wasn't paying enough stamps for the weight of the letter. So I was quite angry because the letter inside looked quite BOSS! I wrote it with my new pen. So I put it away, intending to place another stamp on it later, and just then, it is time for "spring cleaning". So I lost track of the letter.

I have some very good news to tell you Mr. and Mrs. Kohl, I don't feel like repeating the same things I said in the other letter, for more things keep constantly coming in. I passed the test for Music and Art! In fact, I was the only boy in the school who passed. (Don't get the impression that I was the only boy in the school who took the test, because there were more boys who were competing for the test. . . .)

As I said in my last letter about Alvin, I don't really know what's been happening to him, and I haven't been able to get in touch with him. But if you really want to get in contact with him, I can call or visit him and remind upon him that you are still looking forward to seeing some action from him.

As for me, you know how it is. Everything's fine, and I'm doing well in school . . . The weather is just as if it were summertime already. Everyone's in a good mood, and everyone's having a ball! I've received special commendations and I know I will receive more when graduation time arrives. (It is just around the corner.)

So, everything's fine in this country, and I hope that it is likewise in yours, because now, I am enjoying life, and I am hoping that everything keeps working out fine.

Yours truly,
*R. G. Jackson*

I remember the relief and joy I felt reading Robert's last letter—"Everything's fine in this country, and I hope it is likewise in yours." Only I didn't know which country was mine. Spain had begun to feel comfortable. There was the protection of being a stranger and not having to be involved. New York and Harlem were so far away.

Robert's letter as much as anything else seduced me back to the United States. Perhaps I could do some meaningful work.

I arrived back in New York in September and saw Robert almost every week during his first few months in Music and Art; then he disappeared. Three times he failed to show up for appointments, something totally uncharacteristic. I went to Music and Art at eight thirty one morning to meet him before school and see if something was wrong. No Robert— so I asked about him. His teachers hadn't seen him for over a month.

Sad and confused I went to see Robert's guidance counselor, the one person in the school who was supposed to be concerned with his welfare. The guidance office was full of black youngsters doing paper work or waiting to perform meaningless errands. I introduced myself to a small harried lady who winced at Robert's name.

"A bad boy, not the kind we want here. He only came for two weeks. If he doesn't come again we'll have to transfer him."

I tried to argue, to tell her of Robert's talent (which she acknowledged), of his obvious fright, and the support he needed. She shook her head and told me how much experience she had. Then she drew close, pencil in hand and said:

'You know we're very good to — here in this school."

She hastily wrote "Negroes" on a note pad, then rubbed it out as ears perked in the office and eyes rolled at her unperceived.

"The children in this school are very liberal about —"

"Civil rights" appeared and disappeared on her pad.

"But Robert is just not our type of boy, he doesn't fit in."

Robert spent three months in Music and Art. I'm still not sure why he stopped going, but he did and decided to make it on the streets. At that point in his life they offered more than school did.

More what? Perhaps self-respect, money, clothes, friends, and ideology—I don't know. Perhaps Robert suffered white shock and a refusal to face the loss of pride it implied. I do know that after nine years of public school in New York City Robert encountered white individuals of his own age for the first time in high school. Not one or two of them, but an overwhelming number of them, rich, comfortable, sophisticated and liberal, even friendly and jealous. Only he wasn't prepared—maybe it was his poverty, his hypersensitivity—I don't know, I don't know . . . All I could see was that he felt safer on the streets than in school.

Robert is hip, inarticulate. He walks along the street trying to brush away people who happen to stray into his path. He wants to "make it" as a musician—or maybe as a doctor—now it all seems the same to him. School is far away, time and the future mean nothing.

That doesn't mean that this is who Robert "is" once and for all, any more than the fact that he was accepted in Music and Art defined him as a success. Robert is living through experiences he has not been prepared for, no matter how well he has been taught to read, write, or draw.

Recently I gave a course in psychology for a group of high school boys who were interested in the human mind and soul, and its internal and external conflicts. It all started a few months after we returned from Europe. My wife and I were visiting Pamela and her mother, who had become a friend of ours. I had not returned to the New York City Board of Education and was still groping for a way to work with the kids. Pamela's sister, Deborah, was there with her boyfriend. We were talking about the assassination of Malcolm X and the powerful impact of his funeral upon many people in Harlem. I remember Pamela saying:

"Mr. Kohl, it was wonderful, just like President Kennedy. They had it on television and kings and important people were there. A black man buried like that on TV . . ."

We got around to talking about the psychology of assassins and murderers when Deborah's boyfriend challenged me.

"What's psychology anyway—what does it have to do with people?"

I didn't want to be bothered and told him that if he really cared and could find six friends who were interested I would teach them a course about psychology and its relevance to human living.

I didn't think any more of it until he called a week later and told me he had five other people and they were ready to begin. I was flattered and challenged—does psychology, the discipline, have anything to do with human living? Perhaps this was something to offer the kids that could be of use in their lives. I contrived to get an empty room Saturday afternoons at Teachers College where I was

a student in all but heart and spirit, invited Alvin and Robert
to attend, and began to teach once more.

Robert came to the first session and afterwards described
it.

Well, now, I want to talk about the first class that I
took in psychology. Mr. Kohl was teaching us all about the
study of the mind and how people react to certain things and
why people do these things.

We first started on this imaginary human being. Her
name was Anna O and she was having certain problems. She
is a very, very moody person and she is a very quiet, but very
intuitive person and she liked to day dream a lot. At first
it was all right, but at the end her day dreaming starts to
get a little worse, until finally it got so bad that it caused
her to get into a lot of serious trouble.

Now, she liked to dance and go out to parties and
everything, but when her father was finally striken with a
disease she had to stay home and watch. Now, she knew she
had to stay and watch over him, but she didn't want to really,
and, well she just didn't like the idea of it. And so she began to get worried about her father and she began to get
worried about everything else in the past.

By her family being so strict on her she couldn't be
what she wanted to be, she had to be sort of like a puppet or
a doll, something that's represented by her family, by her
parents.

And, all of these tensions caused her mind to kind of
get corrupted in a sort of way and so, she got so worried she
was forced to think that her arm became paralyzed and she
couldn't move her arm. But deep inside she knew she could
move it but she just refused to face reality.

The main thing was she had never been in the right
form of society. She never got around to speaking to a lot
of people and associating with a lot of people. She was always alone in the house and so she began to get hallucina-
tions and everything.

Now, Mr. Kohl was teaching us about this, the thing
is, we wanted to know why she is acting this way.

We gave a few answers and I said that she is just trying
to rebel from her family and she is refusing to face reality.
Some of the guys said, "Well, she just didn't want to force
herself to see that these things that she was dreaming and

everything, wasn't really true." Some of the guys said that
well, maybe she was sick.

Now these are all possible answers, but the main thing
is she needed someone to talk to her. She had never had no
sexual life. She never really had anyone to really sit down
and talk to her.

Finally the doctor had talked to her and this seemed to
calm her down. Her arm didn't hurt her and whenever there
was music playing she stopped coughing and all this. It was
found that perfect supervision by another human being or
by a friend, could help her solve her problems.

Now we studied the mind, the three main parts such
as the ego, the super-ego and the pleasure.

Now, the strongest part of the mind depends on what
kind of person this person is gonna be and it turned out that
Anna's pleasure was turning out to be one of the strongest
parts. But she couldn't fight it, her ego couldn't fight it because her super-ego and pleasures both together were the
strongest parts and they were both battling away at each
other and she couldn't do anything about it and this caused
her to get nervous and everything . . .

We talked about the ego. The ego is you, me, myself
and I, if you want to put it that way, and that's the part of
the mind which . . . it's sort of like your body is sort of like
the outside part of the body, the sort of the frame . . . you
know, like a car. Now say the car has the motor, wheels
and everything, now all you have to do is put on the frame.
That's sort of like the ego, what it is. But, it's not only a
frame, it's you, as sort of like you being a person and you're
using the super-ego and the pleasures. Super-ego and the
pleasures are sort of like your tools and you are using them
. . . but nevertheless, unfortunately, it's hard for a person's
ego to catch, to keep control of his whole mind because
one thing about human being, he can be easily influenced.
His ears and his eyes can be easily exposed to many different
things as he grows older. It is hard for the ego to keep up
with these things, to know what's right, to know what's
wrong, to know what he's doing, to know what not to do, to
know what to do, and everything else like that.

But, mainly, this whole discussion was on the topic of
common sense in general. It is really a nice subject because
I think it is one of the easiest subjects to teach, probably is
the easiest because it deals only with the common sense
and is nothing new to learn and is no mathematical prob-

lems, nothing that you have to remember, it's just you, your-self and your mind and what you do everyday, your everyday life . . . Too many people are scared to face it. Not too many people have that good a common sense to know, to analyze the subject, just as they have analyzed many other subjects like, science, math, and all this. Now if they teach math and science, and even sex in school, why can't plain psychology be taught in school? Why do they have to wait until you take a special course in college, then study about it? See, the thing is that in school they put the subject of psychology in such a way that not too many people like it, not too many people want to study it . . . people won't even learn it be-cause they put it in such a vast and complicated category, and they wait, they don't teach you like they would teach any other simple subject. They wait until you get way in college because they don't think this many people that want to learn it while they're kids and would be influenced by it. But why would they teach kids such a hard thing as math and starting from even the second grade on up, and still can't teach psychology at their age?

Robert didn't return the next week. He disappeared, then appeared twice, and finally disappeared for a year. For some reason he came to see me last Christmas. He brought a friend and we sat over lunch, awkward and embarrassed. His friend was a singer, and they wanted to use my tape recorder to practice and hear themselves. Robert had decided to become a composer and musical organizer. The Motown myth perme-ates his life. A corporation headed by a black man, work without a white boss, independence, money. . . . I listened to Robert talk and thought of my father and my brother, of so many friends and relatives. Making it, making it fast and making it big—somehow the streets were Americanizing Robert. He was no longer interested in art, in developing his talent, because that way was too slow. It wasn't that he ceased to care about art so much as that at this stage in his life he cared more about money. I couldn't object for it was possible that Robert was on the way to an economic resolution of his problems. Yet I couldn't completely buy it either. It is better for Robert to be rich than poor, but how much better? He is making himself hard and ruthless in order to succeed. It has worked before in the United States and may work for Robert, but at what human cost?

For a while Robert returned to Music and Art, though I now understand he will be transferring to another high school in September. He looks with increasing disbelief and cynicism at me, the last white person he can talk to, for an answer, some answer to problems he lives yet is still afraid to articulate. He does not like becoming hard or cruel and suffers it quietly. Yet what solace can I offer, what concrete offer of a life of hope and not hate; what more than the fact that I care, which in this country today he just cannot believe is genuine? Robert lives with the poverty, prejudice, and hatred he described in the sixth grade at the age of twelve, only with four years of reinforcement.

In this school, there aren't any white people, because most whites don't like colored people just because of their color, race, and decendence. The white people take more for themselves, and let the negros have the left overs. Downtown, the whites have all the machines, tall buildings, and beautiful apartments, while the negros live uptown, in harlem, where there's cracked streets, stinky, messy sidewalks, old slums, and no beautiful apartments. It's just like the whites are masters, and the negros are dogs, and the whites take more for themselves, and leave the negros the scraps. I think there should be more integration between the whites and negros.

It is hard to stop writing about Robert—this is not fiction. At no moment does his story cease and by ending my writing of him I inevitably leave a final impression which his life may contradict the next day. That is my hope, and I am glad that I cannot yet say with conviction what Robert will become and who he will be as a man.

Robert is not the only one of the thirty-six children who is now close to being a dropout—John, Margie, Carol, Sam—I stopped searching, don't want to know the full extent of the misery and tragedy of the children's present lives. Recently one of the kids told me:

"Mr. Kohl, one good year isn't enough . . ."

I've lived that truth in lucid detail through the last four years of Alvin's life. He still believes he will make it to college and beyond—or sometimes he believes it—I can't tell since he has closed and hardened inside and is only periodically communicative. He is quite the opposite of Robert in many ways; he refuses the mask of hipness, does not smoke or drink. He is absolutely puritanical in his rejection of the streets and is often fanatical in support of the schools and education. Yet he is not untempted. At this moment he

just cannot put the parts together. His writing, his curiosity
and periodic brilliance, have been no help in school. Teachers have treated him as an illiterate, and when he objected
too cleverly, he found himself classified as a "discipline problem" and "trouble-maker." Recently a guidance counselor in
junior high school tried to force him into a nonacademic program in high school. He refused, but ultimately was admitted
to an academic program. But he arrived in high school stig-
matized, a "bad" boy.

Alvin doesn't like to talk of this subtle, prejudiced un-
dermining of his pride and confidence. He takes it within,
sometimes sulks and comes close to quitting. Only infrequently, and then usually indirectly, does he reach out in
desperation, as he did the year my wife and I were in
Europe. . . .

[Received September 18, 1964]

Dear Mr. and Mrs. Kohl

I am very very sorry that I have not been writing you
recently but I was sort of in a hurry to get so many things
done. I like my new school very much it is much better
than my old one it is well integrated we have many italian,
white, and spanish people in our class, going to school is much
fun now than it was before. How are you, what have you
been doing lately, are you planning to teach this year? I
would really like to know how is Mrs. Kohl give my regards
to Mrs. Kohl. I hope you are having a pretty nice time where
you now I'm having a wonderful time around block today
after school. I hope that will write back soon. I wrote a letter
sending in it a program of the concert but letter was sent
back because of incorrect postage. With my regards.

*Alvin Curry*

December 3, 1964

Dear Mr. Kohl and Miss Judy

I am very sorry that I did not write you recently, but
unfortunately I somehow managed to misplace your last
postcard from Spain, with the correct address on it. Since
you have written this second letter I took the address from
it and that is why I took terribly long to write you. How is
Miss Judy. I know it is kind of late but just the same Happy

thinksgiving. Will you be back in the city for Christmas? there are so many questions that I know you would like me to answer I shall begin as of now! 1. *How am I finding the new school?* Ans. Well for one thing it is *well integrated* which I like very much, we have a *majority* of very nice, highly intelligent teachers like you and Miss Judy. Our school looks almost like —— but it is cleaner and nicer. The principal of our school whose name is Mr. —— is very strict. He insists on perfection from every student in the entire building including teachers as well. My official teacher whose name is Mr. —— who has only been in that school for 1 year, He is too nice of a teacher to us it is very hard for him to get discipline when he needs it. (which is very often) Mr. —— is also my math teacher, he is very kind and gentle he is what I wouldn't call "a fightin man". I am in class 8³-142 (v.t.) vocal talent. 2. *What have I been doing in my free time?* Ans. I have been trying to read a few of those books you have given me, I am now on the book called "Of Mice and Men" I have went to the Brooklyn Branch Library to borrow a few books on: Ventriloquism, Criminology, Crime Detection, and Law. They are very interesting. I have also been riding my bycicle to Prospect Park and along Atlantic Avenue and I saw many things I had never seen before in Prospect Park. I also have been trying to fix up my bike with all the money I can get So far I have 25 cents I hope I will have about $5.00 to buy a pair of brakes But I don't think I can make it because I have to have too much money for lunch in school. I hope you will try to be here for Christmas I miss you. Come here for Christmas if you possibly can. Please! Please write me back as soon as you recieve this letter, And let me know if you can come!

March 13, 1965

Dear Mr. Kohl,

How is Judy. I hope you are feeling fine also, because I am not. I am feeling very strange every time I go to school because there are so many White people there, it is a good feeling. I am not feeling fine because i seem to be disinterested in science. maybe because my teacher doesn't take time to *clerify* and *demonstrate* the problems as you do. If Miss Judy is still painting, ask her to save a few so I may see them. It seems that I do not have a friend in the world now, that you and Miss Judy left for Spain. Please try *without displeasure,*

to come back soon. My mother says she likes your book
very much, I didn't get a chance to read it yet because my
sisters beat me to it. I am also unhappy because *Tippy is no
longer here,* (the lady downstairs when we went out one day
to church, told her husband to take our cat in his car someplace and leave him, and when we came back he was gone
and she said she hadn't seen him, I hate her for that. because
I know she took Tippy somewhere and left him because she
was afraid of cats every since she moved downstairs (her
daughter Marlyn told us and her mother beat her afterwards). I don't know what I am interested in now, but I
know it is not school especially this one. I am trying to think
of a hobby to keep my mind off of other things, can you
suggest one for me?

> sincerely yours
> *Alvin Curry*

    please write soon
my mother gives you her regards!

For a while I believed that Alvin would not write again.
I've been trying to encourage him to complete *The Boy in the
Slums* and convince him of its worth. One night he did sit
down and add to his work.

## CHAPTER 3 A DAY AFTER SCHOOL

Usually after school I would stay in the park or go to the
library in order not to come home and do my work in the house
or homework but this day was very different. Instead of
going to the park or library I went to my house because
I had a spelling test the next day and I wanted to study
just to have something to do because it very easy for me
to get bored without anything to do so I studied for the
test not that I needed it or anything like that you understand it's just that I didn't have anything else to do. Well
anyway I was sort of looking out of the window and all
when I had a wonderful idea . . . why not go down to the
park near my school and watch the dope addicts take
their fixes? . . . this was something that was seen very often
around my block. As I was on the way out to do just this,
I saw my friend James who was very light with dark
black hair and always had an expression on his face saying
where the hell is *Barbara*? where the hell is Alvin and where

the hell is everybody? (he was always looking for somebody or trying not to see a special person he had a fight
with that same day or had borrowed money from.) but I
liked him just the same even if he did owe me money and
was trying to avoid me. So I told James to come and go
with me to the park to go *sightseeing,* and all but he told
me that he couldn't because of his mean aunt who was
very strict which I had the (false) pleasure of meeting,
then I asked him to tell his mother that he had to come
over my house in order to finish a report that was supposed
to be due the next day (she was all for school so I knew
that this would work) I went up with him to tell her this
but I sorta stood behind the door while I talked and she
said okay Alvin I know that you wouldn't lie to me because I know you came from a good family (that's what
I can't understand if people hear that you came from a
good family and that your mother didn't stand for any fool-
ishness schoolwise they believed almost everything you say
without a doubt I just can't understand it.) so even though
James had to be back at five o'clock we went down to the
park and watched this Dope addict it was like watching
a movie or something very interesting like that it kept in
surprise and suspense even though you knew what he was
going to do next and at my age then I thought It was the
greatest thing in the world. That is, what practically everybody my age was doing instead of playing games and all
you would go to the park (because of lack of money for
the movies) and watch the dope addicts take their dope.
After Robert and I left the park at 4:30 we had a half
an hour to fool around or something so we went to my
house to pass some time. My house consisted of 3 crowded
rooms (crowded with furniture on a count there was nowhere to properly put everything) and a kitchen that
shouldn't be called one because it was almost falling down
from lack of proper building facilities or something like
that, well anyway this guy James and me we ate a (after-
school lunch) which consisted of merely toast with butter
and a glass of *koolaid* or sometimes milk (canned) (I hate
that canned milk, I would personally like to see the guy
that made condensed milk, I'd give him a piece of my mind
for trying to be different). After James and I had finished
my skimpy after school lunch (skimpy because of all my
sisters and brothers having to get some and all. Thats what
I hate having sisters and brothers not that I hate them but

its just that the idea of always having to share most everything I have Bugs me a lot), we started for his house because we only had five minutes left and we couldn't think
of anything to do in five minutes so we started to go back
to James house. James house was on this block that looked
like it was filled with all the wanted criminals in the world
and still had room to go. His house itself (the outside) was
better than mine because he had a better stoop, and plumbing
than I did, their was always somebody who compared houses
like me to better stoops all the way down to plumbing.
I swear I never knew why this was so, I guess its just that
when something is better than yours (or almost) you just
have to compare it. When we got inside the hall it looked
like one of those hallways that you would expect to see
things that happened in the park or would expect that any
minute before you made it up the three flights of stairs,
that someone would jump out of the dark shadows, or the
alleyway, and kill you or scare you or something like that.
It was real terrible to go in the hall by yourself especially
if you were a woman or something (that is the reason why
I stuck close to James going up the three flights of stairs).
When we finally reached the door unharmed I was trying
my best not to breathe because of the awful smell that
was in the hallway the smell was like that of urine (if you
know what I mean) it smelled like 25 people a day including dogs and cats came in there to relieve themselves,
like that was the only public toilet on the block, as I thought
of this I felt sorry for the *Super* of the Building for his
job of mopping and all. By this time the door to James
house had been open (with his key that he always lost)
and his Aunt started yelling because she said to be back
at five o'clock and we were back at five after five o'clock,
soon after I looked at James and said hello to his Aunt
I left, because instead of having a expression on his face
"where was everybody" he had a expression saying "Alvin
you'd better go because theres gonna be hell in high water
when you do and I don't want her to think that you didn't
come from a nice family? I was always interpreting James
expressions when I found them interesting.

Soon after I had left James house (because of the expression on his face.) I went home to eat and watch our
television which wasn't playing very good and to fool around
with my chemistry set oh by the way I meant to tell you
that I am very interested in science thanks to Mr. Kohl my

teacher, after doing all of this I went to bed and woke up the next morning about the same time as the other day which wouldve been so If it wasn't for the hit on my rear end by my mother who was always doing that sort of thing in order to wake me up, I went to school and it was the same old routine there, I mean lining up and all and after school James couldn't come out because he was being punished so I went home and did all of my work in the house which was very boring.

## MY KIND OF ARGUMENTS

After I had finished all of my work I thought that I would go down stairs and listen to my mother and sister argue which was very seldom because my mother usually doesn't argue with my sisters she just hits them and punishes them but I guess today that she wanted to hear what my sister Sharon who was 14 had to say well anyway they were discussing the topic of boys and school and how my sister should pay more attention to school rather than boys which she was not doing, when I had got downstairs I realized that they were at the last stage of this discussion because I heard my mother say that the next time that my sister Sharon did this that she was going to hit her and that she won't give my sister any more chances. I always miss the good part of the argument especially when it's something that I like to hear.

## CON EDISON

Ma went down to Con Edison with her best dress (which was really her worst and when she got into the Con Edison Building she looked at all of the employees to see which of them had the kindest looking face and with that she presented her case which was that the lights were $127 dollars and that she only had $100 dollars in which she had to have carfare for my sisters to go to school and money for food so she wanted to know if she could only pay $99.87 (which would make him lose $27.00) the employee needed a little encouragement so my mother took out all of her reciepts including old *paid* light bills which she explain to him was a matter of a coupla thousand dollars they have earned over the past years from her. She also explained that she was a good reliable customer of Con Edison's and that she would give him the 27.00 if

she had it, after this story full of sorrow and truthfulness
finally weakened the employee and the employee agreed to
let my mother pay $99.87 and leave her enough money to feed
us and wash clothes. After this incident I expected my mother
to brag and say how smart she was and all that but instead
she said that the only reason it really happened was that
that man understood about welfare and all and he knew all
of the problems that these people had. (I just can't understand it.)

The brilliance, the intuition, and insight are still there
but the hope is fading. Making it in school seems so difficult
and remote, so many years away, that Alvin is vacillating
between total despair and embracing a total answer to all his
anxieties and uncertainties. Recently, in the name of one
of his sisters, he presented "My Object in Life."

My one and only object in life is to commit suicide at
the age of 14, (you ask me why I wait until the age of
14 . . . . . . well! when I was a little girl I always wanted
to see my name on the front page of the daily newspaper
and I've tried to think of lots of ways to suceed in doing
this and after all of my years of trying to get on the front
page of any newspaper I have only reached one conclusion
and that was what I mentioned earlier to commit suicide
by simply killing my self (well I hope that's the best way
to commit suicide is to kill myself). Oh by the way reader
if you have any brilliant ideas about how I can suceed in
killing myself just write to Bellevue Sanitarium and ask
for the Suicideist in ward 24.

thank-you for your contributions so that I may finally be
on the front page of the newspaper no matter which one it
may be.

signing off: THE SUICIDEST
(*Alias*) *Sheila Curry*

Last summer I tried to get Alvin a job. There were so
many anti-poverty projects about that promised so much
that there seemed no problem. One program, involving work
and a leadership training course, seemed particularly hopeful so I wrote recommending Alvin.

Sir:

I'm writing this letter with respect to our telephone conversation of this afternoon. I spoke to the boy whom I men-

tioned to you and he is grateful for the opportunity to do any kind of work for any salary as long as it would present a challenge to him. He felt that since he has wanted to work with children for a long time your position would provide him with an excellent opportunity.

His name is Alvin Lewis Curry and at present he is entering the tenth grade. His school performance up to now has been erratic, swinging from the brilliant to the indifferent.

If Alvin can get the job, there would be no trouble providing carfare and he said that he welcomes the opportunity to see some of the world outside of his neighborhood.

I would be grateful for anything you could do for Alvin. Thank you very much for offering something in this increasingly desperate and depressing situation.

Yours sincerely,
*Herbert R. Kohl*


Alvin was accepted. I heard nothing until a month and a half later. I called Alvin's mother one day to see how things were going and Alvin answered. He ashamedly confessed that he quit the job, and then as his anger rose he told me that as much as he wanted to work he couldn't take it. After a week of orientation and "leadership" training, he was handed a broom and mop and made an official "junior janitor" for the summer. The humiliation was too much. I told Alvin to forget it, write the whole thing off as some pious mistake of well-intentioned but harmless people who weren't conscious of their prejudice and condescension.

At the end of the summer I received two letters, however, that I couldn't accept complacently. The first congratulated me for my interest in Alvin, the second, addressed (but never sent) to Alvin, praised him for his work.

I had to respond.


Dear _____:

I received your letter and a copy of the one that you sent Alvin. Quite truthfully I cannot understand how you can be so hypocritical and complacent. As far as I understand your training program it seems to me that everything that Alvin was exposed to this summer was a systematic attempt to degrade him. A training program that has the gall to make one of the trainees a "junior janitor" and "allow" him to mop the floors and clean up after everyone else is nothing but another unthinking confirmation of the hope-

lessly inhuman and condescending way that whites in this
poor country automatically think of blacks. Your pleasant
words about Alvin's cheerful face and delightful summer
ring very hollow in front of the simple fact that Alvin quit
your program. That he couldn't tell you this but just allowed himself to disappear is a testimony to his trust and
faith in those who conducted the program. Too many people in the United States are trying to do too much "good"
to others and have failed to look within themselves.

> Yours sincerely,
> *Herbert Kohl*

Several weeks ago Alvin came to my house, and without
a word of greeting went to the typewriter and spent the
afternoon perfecting his lessons.

### * STUDENTS-ENROLLMENT *

*1. Who is the original man?*
The Asiatic Blackman the maker, owner, cream of the planet
earth father of civilization God of the universe.

*2. Who is the colored man?*
Caucasion yakubt-made-devil, skunk of the planet earth.

*3. What is the total population of the original people in the
   wilderness of North America and in all of the world?*
There are 17 million plus 2 million Indians in the Wilderness
of North America. There are 4 billion 400 million in all
the world.

*4. What is the total population of the colored man in the
   W.N.A. and in all of the world?*
There are 103 million 100 thousand colored people in w.n.a.
There are 4 million in all the world.

*5. What is the total square miles of water?*
     139,685,000
*What is the total square miles of the planet earth?*
     196,940,000 squ. miles
*What is the totol square miles of dry land?*
     57,225,000

*6. What is the total sq. miles of useful land used by the total
   population?*
     29,000,000

7. *How much is used by the original man?*
23,000,000

8. *How much is used by the colored man?*
6,000,000

9. *What is the said birth record of the nation of Islam?*
Alpha and Omega (no beginning no end).

10. *What is the said birth record of the nations other than Islam?*
Christianity—551 years old
Buddhist—35,000 years old

He signed his work with his "original" Muslim name. Then I helped him with algebra. We talked about college and the future. He sighed and told me that he hadn't been to school for three weeks.

Alvin had been converted to the Brotherhood, an offshoot of Elijah Muhammed's Black Muslim Temple, in the heart of Medina, only two blocks from his house. For the Brothers, Manhattan is Mecca and Harlem its heart, while Brooklyn is Medina with its heart in Fort Greene. The only lessons Alvin had been studying for many weeks were Muslim lessons on the history of the white devil in the wilderness of North America. They make sense of him, these stories of the white man's cruelty and lies, the spook religion Christianity, with its unknown god and hypocritical promises to the black man of rewards in some future life for patience in bearing the white man's unchristian behavior in this one.

Alvin sees the lies in white man's history as taught in the schools and agrees with the Brothers that history really means *"His* story," white man's tales meant to convince the black man of his inferiority. He knows that when teachers tell of justice in America, they mean "just us," the white man. These verbal games, so much more than games, reflect to Alvin the world as he lives it.

One day, after being abused by a police officer for trying to defend an innocent child from being arrested, Alvin said to me: "Mr. Kohl, you can get arrested for stirring up justice around here."

The Brotherhood is made up of teen-agers for the most part. Many are dropouts. Others, like Alvin, try school, leave in despair, only to return hoping things will be different. Some learn sufficient discipline and self-respect from the Brotherhood to put up with school.

From the outside the Brotherhood may seem like just

another hate group, but it is much more than that to the youths who are members. It is a religion that teaches pride and self-love. It has a written mythology and dogma passed from youth to youth that may well be solving more reading problems than the newest and most sophisticated reading texts. This doctrine preaches rejection of a white world that rejects. It preaches the possibility of a rich and powerful black society, a turning of the tables. This is undeniably dangerous for the white society, but no more dangerous than the white racism that gave rise to it. For Alvin it may not be so dangerous and may even give him a strength and pride that is healthier than his present despair. I say "may," for Alvin seems too sensitive and far too intelligent to accept "total" answers.

If the Brotherhood is of equivocal value to Alvin, I feel myself powerless to help in any way. His personal grief transcends movements, advice, consolation, and even love. At present he sees no place for himself in school, society or in life itself. Recently he wrote:

## THE CONDEMNED BUILDING

There is a leaky faucet, going with a steady drip of water, there is no recreation whatsoever where a person can spend his leisure time, but there is something to look at, the walls which have plaster peeling, which suggests different moods that a person may be in, the walls are so arranged that they suggest different scenes like maybe a scene of you gradually graduating from boyhood to man when the mirage has passed you notice that the windows are uneasily pitch black suggesting for you maybe a private hell, where you can satisfy your own desires. Then your eyes slowly move to the ceiling which suggests a mirage of heaven where you may have a chance to find out the real meaning of life, the windows and the ceiling have a certain contrast between each other which seems to worry you into making a hasty decision, which swiftly moves you to the door with which you step out into the outside, where you ask yourself why is this building condemned, where a person can find his inner self. Why do they condemn this building where man can find out what he is or will be.

Why do they condemn Life.

Ralph also has an original Muslim name, though he finds the Muslim life too restrictive and moral. The last time

I saw him he was wandering about the streets, wearing a top-coat that was a bit too long and too warm for the spring weather. He was beginning to look like those permanent dwellers in junkies' paradise, the homeless men who live on stoops and wander from hallway to hallway. It was hard to talk to him, he seemed so far away from the angry child who wrote *The Nightclub,* who played and joked with Alvin, Maurice, and Michael. I knew it was pointless to ask him about school, but I did anyway. He shrugged his shoulders and told me that it takes so long to get anywhere in school that he just couldn't see the point. It's not that Ralph was any more impatient than a normal middle-class adolescent; rather he couldn't satisfy his normal adolescent needs—decent clothing, money for a few dates and entertainment, those external things that represent adolescent self-respect—while patiently preparing in school to satisfy adult ones. Only the streets seemed to provide the possibility of winning fast money and respect, and Ralph was willing to gamble for them against his young life rather than remain in the limbo that was school.

We only spoke for a few minutes, then Ralph shuffled off. I gave him my telephone number and told him to call if he ever felt the need. There was nothing else to do, and it was always possible that he would get tired of the streets, or want more than they offered. At that moment he would need someone to be there and say that quitting once is not the end, to help him back to himself and his dreams and aspirations. Perhaps I could help by being there to listen to him again.

RECENTLY I saw another of the children for the first time in four years. I was in the hospital with a broken hip where one of the other patients told me about an unusual newspaperboy who wanted to be a writer. The hospital was only three blocks from my school so naturally I was curious and asked to see the boy. It was Michael, who, when last I saw him, was still working on his novel *Frankenstein Meets Cyclops and Psyche,* a wild, original blend of Greek myth, street violence, and horror movies. I never saw the finished product, and Michael reluctantly admitted that the book was never finished. He hadn't written since the sixth grade, was never provided with an opportunity to do so in school, and was too busy working or too preoccupied with personal and family problems to write. Yet, four years later, he still dreamed of being a writer.

I was surprised and thrilled, and encouraged him to write again. He asked me what he could write about, and I told him to think of what he cared about. Our first conversation was brief: Michael had to deliver his papers to the other patients in the hospital. The next morning he visited me, presented me with a free copy of the *Times,* and said he would have something that evening. He didn't but the next morning he left a notebook on my bed and apologized.

"I'm sure it's no good, maybe you shouldn't read it."

Later I looked at the title and Michael's brief description of his work: "*The Pit of Hell* by Michael Earle, the story of a young teen-ager who drops out of school and tries to make a living without an education by jeopardizing the lives of the people who loved him."

The story is just unfolding. I see Michael every few weeks now. He has finished the first chapter and works in fits and starts. He is attempting a more difficult and dangerous work than the Frankenstein book, one that presents clear and immediate parallels with his present life.

Michael has not dropped out of school, but he has been tempted. Perhaps this novel is his way of experimenting with the future, or of communicating his doubts and anxieties to me. But it is also more than that—Michael wants to be a writer. He has rewritten the first chapter of *The Pit of Hell* three times and has asked me to be ruthless and honest about his work. He wants to master the craft and seems to have the patience and persistence to do it. With luck he may make it as a writer, whatever he decides about school which seems irrelevant to his life and education.

GRACE has been luckier than many of the other children in a way, though not without a cost to herself. She was the only child in 6-1 to go to a "Special Progress" class in a junior high school in another part of the city. Her test scores were good enough for this even before she entered my class. Because of her selection, Grace was separated from her friends, and within her new school from pupils who weren't considered to be "gifted." For two years she was groomed to succeed. She had a full academic program, overloaded with facts and skills guaranteed to put one through entrance examinations. She was converted to the gospel of grades and rushed nervously into competition. I saw her lose interest in her old friends, become tense and ambitious. She was preoccupied with success, and fully taken up with school. As her letters to my wife and me in Spain testified, it paid off.

Sept. 18, 1964

Dear Mr. and Mrs. Kohl;

Sorry I couldn't write sooner, but my father was just discharged from the hospital and it took some time to get straightened out.

How is Paris? Is it really romantic and enchanting. Did you see the Eiffel Tower?

I've started a stamp collection with your Parisian stamps, and the two English stamps my pen-pal sent me today.

I am in 8$^{sp}$, and Honor League[1], and a school patrol[2].

My official teacher rules with an iron hand. In science, the lessons on genes and chromosomes came in very handy. The encyclopedias were even handier for my first report.

I hope you return soon. Must close now before I have to use extra stamps for over weight.

> Your everlasting student
> and student-n-law,
> *Grace*

P.S. So far I have two commendations. 1—an honorable organization where one must have 85 average and A in conduct
2—superior officers. (monitors)

Octo. 15, 1964

Dear Mr. and Mrs. Kohl,

Since you are in Spain, I think it's very appropriate to write this letter in Spanish. Don't look so alarmed. The translation is on another page . . . in the letter.
(translation)

How are you? I hope you are well. Do you like Spain? I am well, my brother and sisters are well, and my father doesn't have to go to the hospital because he has been there already and when he returned, the doctor said that he doesn't have to return.

I am doing well in school, especially Science. I have a B+ on my Shakespeare report, a B on my first Social Studies Homework, but a A (99% in red ink). My Spanish teacher says that I am very intelligent. Do the men and women dance in the street? Do you hear the Beatles in Spanish or English (with love from me to you, Do you want to know a secret?) We don't hear their records now.

I will be writing to you in the near weeks.

> Yours   truly,
> *Grace*
> Until   later.

Dec. 18, 1964

Dear Mr. Kohl and Judy,

I have received your gift. It's lovely. It's the first Imported, genuine thing I have ever known. But I'm sorry to say that I might not have nothing to put in it for quite a while. My father just came out of the hospital Thursday (Dec. 17, 1964). He was in for the operation he was supposed to get in the summer. This Christmas will be a shaky one for us, but having him home is steady enough for me. Because of his illness, I was unable to buy you a present, but I do have a Christmas card for you (smell it) my sister's personal smelling salts (and it does smell).

GUESS WHAT??!!

I have been chosen with some other girls in my class (8-313ˢᵖ), according to reading level, to attend Mt. Holio in Massachusetts. It is a school where the *girls* attend for 8 weeks of the summer in courses of Math, English, S.S., Science, etc. This way they will tell how well we are doing in certain areas than other areas. On Feb. 6, we will take the test. On Jan. 21, the test for Bronx High School of Science. I am going to take it. I hope I pass both.

My first marking period marks are:

> English  85
> Math    88    S.S.   85
> Science 90    Lang.  98

A *"98"* in Spanish. Good by   Yours truly,   *Grace*

Feb. 13, 1965

Dear Mr. Kohl and Judy,

I hope you recieved my Christmas card. How did you spend your Christmas? I had a good one. I got the game of Monopoly, an album, a box of Helena Robinstine Dusting Powder, (not for dusting furniture), and a pair of *hand* knit bedslippers with a pair of silken pajamas. (yellow) I played monopoly on Christmas from 10:20 (day) (when I came home from church) to 2:00 the next morning.

We had our midterms on the 12th of Jan. to the 15. Math and science are my ideal. On Science I got a 102 on my test. On Social Studies I got a 87. In english, I got a 89. In math I got a 96 and on my spanish midterm I got a 100 (the highest you. could get) My math level is 10.0 (the highest on that test.)

We got our report cards Wed. 2/10/65. My marks:

Math 90      Sci. 95
Eng. 90      Foreign Language: 98
S.S.  90      My average: 92⅗

I got your book. I love it. I took it to school. My teacher thought it quite nice.

Signing off<br>Your pupil: Grace

P.S. Write Soon!

P.S.P.S. I took the test for the special schools in New England, last saturday 2/6/65. Results will be back in 6 or 7 weeks.

May 5, 1965

Dear Mr. Kohl,

Sorry I haven't written you in such a long time but I was too busy with High School. We are graduating this year from the 8th grade. I sent. in an application to bronx H.S. of Science. And a lot of other applications to other schools for my second choice school If I didn't get H.S. of Science. I haven't heard from the other people at the private schools yet but I still have hope. I got my report card my grades:

Math: 92      S.S.:  90
Sci.:  95      Lang.: 95

My Spanish teacher lowered my Spanish grade 3 points for the 3 days I didn't bring in my money for my spanish notebook so she gave me a —1 for each day I didn't bring in my money ($1.50) Could I help it if I didn't have the money? And I wasn't gonna steal it to please her. I didn't get an English mark because I didn't hand in a ha-ha number of ha-ha reports and homeworks. ha-ha The Honor League assembly is Friday and I'm In it. I have a 93 average and got an A in conduct. The test for Bronx H.S. of Science was April 13, 1965, Tuesday. (Good thing it wasn't a Friday)

GUESS
### WHAT ! ! ! ? ? !

Today in science (4th Period) the head of Guidance dept. sent a boy for us. When we got down I was a new member of the Bronx High School of Science. Yep!

You read right and no need to read it again. I passed the test. Me, Daisy, Henry, and James Ratleff. All the others, failed (so to speak) already 2 people have been accepted to the priviate High Schools. When Miss —— told me I went mad. screaming and yelling and jumping all over the place. Mommy didn't believe me when I called her from the office and told her. We have a term paper due from May 10-14. Mine is due on May 12. It has to be on a famous person. I'm doing Joan of Arc. It has to be no less than 25 pages.—typewritten.

Signing off now
Your pupil *Grace*

P.S. I really passed the test for High School of Science.

June 24, 1965

Dear Mr. Kohl and Judy,

I thank you very, very, very, much. I received it on the 24 and I graduate on the 25. THANK YOU

THANK YOU    THANK YOU

I P
   A
     S
       S
         E
           D!

I PASSED!
   I PASSED!
      I PASSED

I will be going to a *private school* in the fall. On July 1st I will be going to Mt. Holyoke College, South Hadley, Mass. in preparation for the school in the fall. I will be going to the —— School in the fall. They've giving me a
$13,000
scholarship for 4 yrs. ($3250 yr.) We could write each other until you come home. You'll return on the 22 and I'll return on the 26 of August. HAPPY!   HAPPY!   HAPPY!

I PASSED      I PASSED      I PASSED
the address for my summer preparation school
                    Mt. Holyoke College
                    South Hadley
                    Massachusetts

                                    Your pupil Grace

(I'm so excited I can't spell straight) Thank you again: Bye

Dear Mr. Kohl,

I'm having fun! fun! fun! All you do is go to classes,
eat, sleep, ride your bike and go to activities. This after noon
my activities are Dance (Modern) and swimming. I learned
to swim and ride a bike while I was here. last weekend (the
10 and 11), we went to Cape Cod. We had a cook out and
we had a campfire. (I was in charge) This weekend (18, 19)
we went out again. On Sunday we went to Tangle wood to
hear the BOSTON SYMPHONY ORCHESTRA. then on Saturday
evening at 8:30 at Cinema 1 and 2, a swanky movie house,
we saw, hold on to your hats, MY FAIR LADY!! It was the
most umptiously, beautiful, movie I ever seen. In fact its the
only movie I've ever seen. Expect another letter in about 5
days. I have to end this one because I'm expected for my
dance class in 7½ minutes and there's *so much* to tell you.

                                    Bye Love Grace

Now Grace is in her second year in a New England
Prep School. She fits wholly neither there nor at home in
Harlem. She is one of the "school Negroes," a gifted one but
still an anomaly. The other students are as open as possible,
and she has made several sincere friends. Yet to live simultaneously in two worlds, a rich white one and a poor black
one, is to be fully a part of neither. Grace has become
alienated from Harlem, her home, her friends, her very self,
in attempting to be part of the prep school world. But she
can't fully participate there; she's too poor, too lonely, too
much of a special case. It is hard to know what will come
of her alienation, whether it will pull her apart or whether
she will transcend it and show us adults a way to synthesize
the contradictions we make and allow in our society. It is
equally difficult to know whether her alienation is any better
or healthier than Robert's, or Alvin's.

Grace used to be friendly with Pamela, and recently I
tried to bring them together. It was an awkward, even hostile,
encounter. Pamela lives in Harlem, knows who she is, and

is proud of her color and life. She was one of the quieter children in 6-1, yet one of the most respected. I noticed that no one bothered her though she was small and seemed so fragile. In June of that year I found out why. Brenda W., one of the bigger and tougher kids, tried to bully Pam, who listened for a minute, then slammed her books to the floor and went for Brenda. There was such justice and fury in her assault that Brenda wilted, as I am sure I would have. This hard, just core of Pamela's has remained unchanged, though she has blossomed into a beautiful young woman. Now she works for Haryou, protesting some of the outrages the Harlem community is subjected to. She is not bitter or desperate, but she is very angry. The balance she maintains between social anger and personal joy I have seen nowhere else.

But Pamela and Grace are worlds apart. There is little joy in Grace's present ambiguous existence and too much suppressed anger. She can't know whether to love or hate Pamela's Harlem or the white downtown world of her prep school classmates. She can't think of all the contradictions in her present life if she is to continue it, and she feels she must. She is convinced of the value of education and will push herself to college, perhaps further if she isn't overtaken by all she must forget, suppress, hide. Pamela and Grace can't talk, and now Grace and I can't talk. It became clear a year ago that she wasn't interested in seeing me. Perhaps she was afraid: whatever it was, I quietly dropped out of her life. It's ironic; the child who has made it in school is the one I can least communicate with.

There is no point in continuing to document each child's problems and pains. Enough has already been said. The thirty-six children are suffering from the diseases of our society. They are no special cases; there are too many hundreds of thousands like them, lost in indifferent, inferior schools, put on the streets or in prep schools with condescension or cynicism. When I think of my work as a teacher one of the children's favorite myths, that of Sisyphus, continually comes to mind: the man condemned to roll a rock up a mountain only to see it fall back to the bottom, to return to the bottom himself and take up his unending task. Without hope and without cynicism, I try to make myself available to my pupils. I believe neither that they will succeed nor that they will fail. I know they will fight, falter, and rise again and again, and that if I have the strength I will be there to rejoice and cry with them, and to add my little weight to easing the burden of being alive in the United States today.